Looking for Love online

How to Meet a Woman Using an Online Service

Richard M. Rogers

Macmillan • USA
Macmillan Reference
A Simon & Schuster Macmillan Company
1633 Broadway
New York, NY 10019-6785

To my little doll, Karen

Macmillan General Reference
A Simon & Schuster Macmillan Company
1633 Broadway
New York, NY 10019-6785

An ARCO Book

Manufactured in the United States of America

10 9 8 7 6 5 4 3 2 1

Library of Congress Cataloging-in-Publication Data: 96-080105

ISBN: 0-02-861514-X

Editor: Jennifer Perillo
Production Editor: Phil Kitchel
Designer: Amy Peppler Adams—designLab, Seattle

Table of contents

3 Defining Your Goals 21

Let's Sign On—And Cruise 33

Introduction

When I was asked to appear on a national talk show more than two years ago with a woman I had met online to talk about how to meet women using a computer, I thought it would be rather fun. After all, not many people get to go on a talk show, and my lady and I wanted to share the wonderful love we had found and the way it all worked.

By that time, I had logged thousands of online hours, had spoken to hundreds of people and knew that many of them had found mates online. All of us in the online community knew that, when properly understood and utilized, the online environment could provide a safe, effective and practical way of meeting someone with whom you could form a successful day-to-day relationship.

Sadly, the host was more interested in the sexual aspects of online life than the relationship possibilities. Fortunately, the audience was somewhat more enlightened. Undaunted, I appeared on another national talk show about a year later, with practically the same results.

Although there is still some misperception about what goes on in the online environment, I think we've come a long way from those early unenlightened days when one might actually be embarrassed to admit he or she met a mate via a computer. Today, it is a widely accepted and acceptable thing to do. Judging from the number of books on the subject, cyber romance has, indeed, come out of the closet and may be on the way to becoming the single most popular means of meeting a potential spouse.

Still, there is no book written for men—the vast majority of us in the online community—that discusses, in practical, no-nonsense terms the methods and techniques a sincere man can employ to facilitate his search for the right woman.

Since men outnumber women four to one in the online world, there can be considerable competition among us. All you have to do is to look over the shoulder of a woman who's signed on to an online service and witness the number of messages she gets within minutes of entering a chat area to verify that. This book is written to help you contact a woman successfully, maturely, and in a way that will make all your conversations with women online far more enjoyable and fruitful.

I've also written this book as a way to express my own happiness with the woman I met online and to let you know that you, too, can find that same happiness. There are a lot of wonderful women out there in the online world who would like to meet you. I would like that, too. Of course, although this book is written for men, I do hope women will find something in it for them as well—if only that there are plenty of good men looking for you and if you haven't given the online environment a try, perhaps you should.

If you haven't yet experienced the potential for romance that exists in the online environment, you might find it difficult to understand how two people who have yet to meet can possibly develop feelings for each other. It might seem unreal and even a little ridiculous. And yet, I think by the end of this book you'll understand that not only is it possible, it may even be desirable. This has the weight of historical precedent on its side. Not too long ago, men and women formed deep relationships through the exchange of letters. The use of a computer to find a mate is the modern counterpart to that past romantic time.

But the computer provides so much more flexibility than the mere exchange of letters. Through live interactive chat in conjunction with the exchange of e-mail and telephone contact, you and the potential lady of your dreams will have the ability to get to know each other on a very deep level. Each stage in the process—the online stage, the telephone stage, and the meeting stage—brings with it a new level of excitement and anticipation. I don't believe any other type of courtship is quite like it.

Of course, before you get to any of those stages, you'll first have to meet a woman by cutting through the considerable competition. I hope that's where *Looking for Love Online* will help you.

The first part of the book discusses the online environment and looks at the potential it has for finding romance. Even if you're already a member of an online service, you might not be fully aware of everything out there. The chat areas alone can be confusing and intimidating, and appear, at first glance, not to offer very much. I was a member of an online service for six months before I even ventured into its chat area because I thought the people in there couldn't have much of a life if they were wasting it talking to other people. Didn't they know online services were for serious stuff like research? Boy, was I wrong.

The next part of the book delves more deeply into interactive chat and the ways of meeting a woman through this method. We'll take a look at some practical approaches and techniques that you can use and we'll discuss what women want and, equally important, what they don't want.

The rest of the book follows a relationship through the three stages I mentioned above: the online stage, the telephone stage, and the meeting stage. We'll discuss the relative importance of each stage in this developing relationship and how you can successfully progress from one stage to the next. And, yes, there is a discussion about cybersex and the wisdom of pursuing a relationship that centers around cybersex.

Here's hoping that your adventure into this exciting world will be as filled with success, happiness, and love as my own.

acknowledgments

There are always more people involved in a book than the author who appears on the cover, and this book is no exception. Authors devote this page to thanking those people by name. But my first thanks must go to the thousands upon thousands of nameless people who are the true inspiration of this book. Those are the people who make the online environment a vibrant and exciting place and without whom, a book like this would not be possible.

Of those who have helped me directly, I would like to thank my agent, Bert Holtje, who always believes in my ideas and always finds the right place for them; Barbara Gilson, my editor at Macmillan for being understanding and for sculpting this book into its final form; and my special thanks to Karen Kingsbury, who not only acts as my personal editor but is also my partner in life and the direct inspiration for this book.

I also appreciate the kind assistance I received from the online services and others in the online community. I wish I could have contacted all the online services, but that would have been impractical. I'm sure every one would have been as helpful as those I spoke to. Specifically, my thanks to America Online, CompuServe, EchoNYC, Prodigy, and the folks at Match.com. And, finally, thanks to Karl Jack, my friend and owner of Cultural-Connections Online, for his technical assistance.

the online playground

To paraphrase an old love poem,
"How do I meet thee? Let me count the ways."

How many ways are there to meet a woman? For the modern male, there are all too few. Most of the traditional ways—family, friends, church socials—seem to have vanished as our society has become more mobile. The result has been a social paradox: more freedom coupled with an increased sense of isolation.

The "singles scene" replaced the church social as one of the chief places to meet a member of the opposite sex. Whole industries sprang up to cater to our natural desire to meet someone compatible. But bars soon become tiring, and they're not necessarily the best place to meet a woman. Get-away clubs are expensive and you don't get your money back if there are no women getting away that weekend. Health clubs are promising, but you have to pump a lot of iron before the women who frequent them give you more than a sympathetic glance.

Some years ago there was a newspaper article about the ideal place to meet a woman. Where was it? The supermarket. Has it really come down to that? Is the cabbage-patch section of your local grocery store the only place left to find a woman? It's a novel idea, but it also says a lot about the challenges of meeting a woman in our modern society.

Many men turn to the workplace. But romance on the job can be awkward. If the romantic relationship ends, it might be difficult to continue the professional one. And today's legal complications make approaching a woman at work an uncertain proposition. Many sincere men are confused about the difference between trying to engage a woman socially and sexual harassment. Even the most innocent remark can be misconstrued or manipulated, resulting in the loss of face, disciplinary action, or the end of a career. Clearly, the cost of pursuing an office romance often outweighs the benefits.

There are always the newspaper personals, but, if you're like me, you find ads too static, lacking the interactive qualities and immediacy of actual contact. The whole process feels too much like applying for a job. The same is true of match-making services. Personally, I don't like the idea of being "matched" based on some questionnaire. Neither method offers the opportunity to really get to know a potential mate in any meaningful way before you meet.

Not for Nerds Anymore

So, how many ways are there to meet a mate? Today's complicated world poses new challenges in your search. Fortunately, every new challenge has a new solution. And the solution could be right at your fingertips. It's called a computer, and, when attached to a modem, it can open up a whole new way of meeting the woman of your dreams. That's right—the computer is not for nerds anymore!

The diverse world of online services is providing thousands of men just like you with the opportunity to interact live, flirt, and form relationships with women from around the corner to the other side of the world. Sound incredible? It is. And it sure beats the singles scene—and the supermarket. I'll explore all the techniques you can use to make your online excursions exciting and successful. But, before we get into the specifics, a comparison between a "real-life" singles spot and an online one may help you better understand the diversity and levels that different online services offer.

Imagine it's Wednesday evening and you'd like to find a date for Saturday night. You jump in your car and drive to a local hot spot. If you meet anyone at all, chances are pretty good she'll be a woman from your area. Now imagine driving to the local singles scene and having just as good a chance of meeting a woman from your area as out of your area. *Then* imagine that your local singles scene is regularly visited by women from anywhere on earth.

2

To a certain extent, the online world is like that. There are services that are mainly local, some that have a mix of local people and people from all parts of the country, and then there's the Internet, which is visited by people from all over the world. Where you ultimately decide to "drive" to is your choice, and this book won't try to steer you in any particular direction. Rather, this book will help you find that special woman wherever you go.

Although I mention some online services by name in this book, it is only to demonstrate a particular technique. I do not endorse one over the other. They all have their strengths and weaknesses. Perhaps you're already a member of an online service that you enjoy. If not, plenty of online services offer free-trial periods. So, take advantage of the free test drive, kick the tires, and see what service is right for you. Today's online services don't require a lot of technical know-how, just a free program disk (supplied by the service), a modem, and a credit-card number. That's it!

To steer you in the right direction, the following section describes the different types of services available, and highlights the strengths and weaknesses of each in pursuing the goal of this book: finding and meeting a woman online!

The Local Scene

A *bulletin board service* (BBS) is usually populated by people from your town or city. Many are run right out of the owner's home from a personal computer (PC) that's not much different from the one you're using. Some are quite sophisticated, sporting the same colorful displays and ease-of-use features you find in the major online services.

This type of service can range in size from a few citizens to a few thousand. A BBS is like a small town. If you spend enough time on it, you'll probably meet everyone who belongs to it. The *sysop* (system operator) may even contact you while you're online and talk to you. Quite a few have a specific theme or topic, ranging from the ordinary to the erotic, so their populations tend to be homogenous or focused. Because of this, a BBS can be an excellent place to meet someone with the same interests as you.

If you live in or around a large urban area, the chances are good you'll find a BBS worth looking into. The fact that the women you meet will be from your area may be a big advantage. But if you want a bigger place with more diversity and action, a commercial online service is where you want to be.

The Big Scene

The commercial *online services*, like America OnLine, CompuServe, and Prodigy, are much, much bigger than your local BBS. Even the smallest of these has a population of more than two and a half million people. That's larger than many cities! However, an online service is much more diverse than a city. On any of these services, you can just as easily meet a woman from across the country as one from around the corner. You can't say that about most cities. Some services even have international outlets, so it's possible to meet a woman from Canada or Europe.

While these services are big (you'll never meet everyone on them), every service is divided into smaller areas, each with its own focus and theme. You can think of these services as a collection of BBSs, or towns that you can travel between with the click of a mouse button. You can even talk to many people from different towns at the same time. In addition, a commercial online service usually offers a wider variety of things to do. Of course, we're not interested in reading the *New York Times* online, are we? Still, these services got big because they offer so much—all for the same local call that it takes to sign on to a BBS.

If the commercial online services are still not big enough for you or you want to regularly meet women from other parts of the world, then the Internet is the place for you.

The Really Big Scene

No one really knows for sure how many people are on the Internet, but the best estimate is that there are at least 30 million from around the world. That's already more people than many countries have—and it's growing.

In most cases, you reach the Internet through an *Internet service provider* (ISP) that plugs you directly into the "Net." In addition, all of the commercial online services provide Internet access, but if all you want is no-frills Internet, which is quite a lot by itself, ISPs have better

4

pricing structures than the majors. No matter how you get there, once you're on the Net, you'll find it teeming with life and activity. But, unlike the well-organized commercial online services, the Internet can seem chaotic and intimidating for the newcomer. The reason is that the Internet is a collection of computers located all over the world, networked together with no single entity in charge.

If you have the patience and can stand a few wrong turns along the way, the Internet offers one of the most economical, varied, and interesting ways of meeting women. International Relay Chat (IRC), for example, has, on any given day, more than 2,400 *chat rooms* where you can talk with members of the opposite sex. The World Wide Web has many pages devoted to romance, including a plethora of dating and match-making services.

In the next chapter, I'll give you an inside look into chat rooms and other online methods available to finding the woman of your dreams. But whatever service you eventually sign on to—BBS, commercial online service, or the Internet—the possibility and the potential of meeting a woman, perhaps that special woman, is right at your fingertips. Best of all, you don't have to get in your car and drive anywhere—you can do it from the comfort of your own home.

You Can Do It All

Superman can travel faster than a speeding bullet; you can travel faster than that through these online towns. Ultimately, it makes no difference which service you choose because once you discover the speed and comfort with which you can meet people, make contacts, and find friends and, most important, lovers in this remarkable online hunting ground, you may never venture into a singles bar again.

But let's go back to that singles place again to point out some interesting differences between this "real-world" place and the one you'll learn about in this book. Imagine being able to say hello simultaneously to every woman in a singles bar. I suppose this is theoretically possible, if you shout at the top of your lungs, above the music and conversation, *"Hello, every woman in here!"* But I don't think you'd get much response. At the most, you might get some sympathetic stares. More than likely, the women around you would take a couple of steps away.

In the online world, though, you can say hello to everyone at once. Just type, "Hello, everyone," and everybody in the room will see it. When you "walk" in, the chances are good that a conversation will already be in progress, and usually a number of conversations will be going on at the same time. The dialogue, known as *chat*, will scroll quickly on your screen. This might seem a little confusing at first, but you'll soon figure it out and be able to pick up the threads of the different conversations. Feel free to join in. Feel free to ask a question. Feel free to start your own conversation. Or, at the beginning, you may just want to sit and observe the action. It's all right there in front of you on your computer screen; all you have to do is start typing.

Let's take this analogy with the real world one step further. Let's say that by some magic apparatus, you're in a room with 10 women and you can have a private conversation with each of them at the same time, without any of the women knowing about the other conversations. That would be pretty incredible if you could do that in the real world, wouldn't it? Imagine the time it would save—and the expense. In a singles club, you can only approach one woman at a time. You might spend anywhere from five minutes to the whole evening with one lady, only to discover she's not what you're looking for, or vice versa.

This book doesn't guarantee that you will never waste an evening online, or that you will never face rejection, but it *will* help you cut through the considerable competition for women online and increase your odds of finding a date.

Online scenarios are entirely different from the singles-club scenario. The first reason is that the magic of online communications allows you to talk privately to one, three, 10 or as many women as you can manage—all at the same time. This is a considerable timesaver in your search for the woman who's right for you. It can also be a lot of fun. It helps if you are a quick thinker, a fast typist, and good at covering your tracks, especially if you slip and send love and kisses to Marie but they wind up on Brenda's screen! The fact is, you can meet an uncountable number of women in any given evening. The only limit is the size of the service you join and how fast you can think on your toes—or, in this case, your fingertips.

The second reason is that many of the rooms have specific themes and/or topics. This automatically gives you something to talk about. You don't have to grope around nervously for something to say.

The third reason is that on just about every service, every person you meet online leaves you a calling card, in the form of their e-mail name. So, if you find that special woman and she doesn't warm up to you right away, or she seems to be overloaded with other conversations, you can always send her a nice introductory letter that she can read at her leisure.

Let's imagine that all the women you meet in the real world have little placards pinned to their lapels stating their marital status and their interests. That would certainly be a help, but, unfortunately, that isn't the case. Before I started using an online service, the second place my eyes went when I saw a woman I wanted to meet was that ring finger on the left hand. Was there an engagement ring, a wedding ring? If that little gold band was there, it told me she was married.

But not all married women wear wedding rings. Nor do women with boyfriends have any special signs that signify an attachment. I have certainly found myself in social situations with a number of apparently unattached women, struck up a conversation with one, spent some time trying to find mutual interests, and was just about to ask her for a date when she says something to the effect of, "My boyfriend likes that, too." Boyfriend? Why didn't she say that an hour ago!

In the virtual world many people do wear placards on their lapels. They're called *profiles* and one of the things people put in them is their marital status. That is certainly a help. And if they're not wearing a placard, it's acceptable online etiquette to ask at the very beginning if she is married or attached. Is everyone honest? Do people say they're single when they're not? Sure they do. They do that in real life, too.

Fantasy or Reality?

Cyberspace refers to the collection of all the towns we pass through when we enter the world of online communications. Another term often used to describe this world is *virtual reality*. While virtual reality is something that technically requires equipment, such as a head-mounted display, the term has been broadened and is often used to describe what happens online among people.

Virtual reality as used in the first sense is something that appears real but is definitely not. In contrast, what you do, say, and experience when you sign on to a service is not a simulation of reality. It *is* reality. This blurring of the distinction between virtual reality and reality is what gets people into trouble online. For some reason, there are those who are lulled into a false sense of security by the fact that they are sitting in their own homes, hidden behind a computer screen. But the same rules that apply to your "real" life should apply to your online life.

The people you talk to online are not imaginary. Just like you, they come with their own set of strengths and weaknesses. Just like in the real world, some people lie, but most tell the truth most of the time. It is often stated that because of the anonymity of online life, people tend to lie more. That has not been my experience. People are people. A person does not suddenly turn into a psychopathic liar the moment he or she travels to cyberspace. Nor does that person become an angel.

Will a woman lie about her age and weight to a man she meets online? Probably. But it is not uncommon for a woman to do that in real life. Will a man lie about his income or his height to a woman he meets online? Probably. But it is not uncommon for a man to do that in real life. Of course, just as in real life, when you lie, the truth will eventually come out, so it is always better to be up-front from the start.

If you ever peruse the personal advertisements in many newspapers, I'm sure you wonder how all these beautiful women and successful men are still single after all these years. We accept that the people in these ads are not always what they claim to be. We all try to put our best foot forward when meeting strangers. It's no different online.

Rarely do we hear the other side of that coin—that because of the anonymity of online life, people tend to open up more. In the days when drinking was fashionable, it was often said that bartenders had to be part psychologist because absolute strangers would walk up to them, have a few drinks, and tell them the most intimate details of their lives. Then walk out and never be seen again. I am often amazed how women can open up online, especially if you approach them in the right way.

The following chapters discuss the nuts and bolts of how to meet women online, find that special one (if that's what you're looking for), and form a relationship that will eventually be consummated in real life. In my opinion, no better medium has been devised with more potential than the online medium. Through weeks or months of online contact, followed by phone conversations, you can really get to know a woman and form a deep relationship with her. There is no place on earth where you can have a multi-level courtship and get to know and romance a woman for the first time in three different ways: once online, once on the phone, and once in person. It can truly be a marvelous experience.

My experience—and that of millions of people who sign online daily to chat, meet mates, or just play the field—has been overwhelmingly positive. I'm sure yours will be, too.

So, get ready, fasten your seatbelts and be prepared for what could turn out to be the fastest ride of your life as we venture onto this super-highway, this diverse universe, this online playground.

Happy Hunting!

online Hot spots 2

There's a whole cornucopia of places to meet a woman in the online universe and we'll look at them in this chapter. Since this book concentrates on the interactive means of finding the woman of your dreams, we'll cover those areas first, then go into further detail about them in subsequent chapters. But the online universe has something for everyone, so even if you're shy by nature or don't want to talk to people directly, there are still ways to locate and meet a woman. This chapter takes a look at those areas, too.

Live Interactive Chat

The most provocative, immediate, and intense method of meeting a woman is by engaging her in live online chat. As you'll see in the following sections, there's a lot of chatting going on and a lot of ways to do it.

Chatting in Public Rooms

All of the major services have live chat facilities; on the Internet, it's called *international relay chat* or IRC. Chat takes place in rooms, channels, or whatever the particular service you subscribe to may call it, but the principle is pretty much the same everywhere: You "walk" into a defined area filled with people and start talking. No matter what online service you use, rooms tend to have certain themes, so you'll find people who are interested in that particular topic. Usually the room topic is displayed, so you know what you're getting into before you enter, or you may be able to monitor the room from the outside to see if the conversation is interesting.

Topics range from the usual to the esoteric, but make no mistake about it: The most popular topic is sex and romance, in all its various forms and guises. The online environment, as you'll soon discover for yourself, is an extremely liberated one. But, really, all the sex talk online is nothing more than people looking to meet other people and have a good time. These rooms are excellent meeting places, but even those rooms that you'd never talk about sex in, like Christians Online, are great places to meet and find a woman. It's just that if you enter Christians Online, make sure you know something about Christianity and are looking for a Christian woman.

Chat rooms can be wild places where many individual conversations are going on at the same time, in addition to a general conversation. You get involved by typing something, pressing a key, and seeing your words appear on the screen along with everyone else's. It takes a little practice to follow the conversation, or, sometimes, to even know if someone is responding to you or to someone else. Things can happen pretty fast and you have to be quick on your feet, or, in this case, your fingers. But you'll soon get the hang of it and feel right at home.

You'll notice that women tend to be pretty popular in chat rooms. As soon as they walk in, they're greeted with a lot of hellos— and sometimes more pointed comments. I once tried an experiment: I asked a woman to create a public chat room on one of the commercial online services. In a matter of minutes, her room was populated with several men, all seeking to make her acquaintance. I also created a public chat room—and sat there all by myself. So, I closed up shop and went into her room. Considering that online services are still 85 percent male, this should come as no surprise.

The other thing you'll notice about chat rooms is that they are populated by a core group of people who seem to be in the room at the same time day after day and visitors who just drift in and out, whom you may see once and never again. The regulars are crucial to the life and sustenance of every chat room. Many of them have been in the same rooms for years and know each other both online and have often met in the physical world.

It's good to get to know these individuals and, perhaps, to become a regular yourself. It can really make a chat room feel like home, especially when you walk in and all the women send you cyber hugs and kisses and all the men say hello. It's a nice feeling to be welcomed. It also provides an excellent check against all of those bad things the media are so fond of warning us against. We've all heard the horror stories—kids posing as adults, the ever-present con person, men posing as women—and we know it's the media's job to bring us the bad news, but I do have to wonder if any of these reporters have ever spent more than three minutes online.

There's no question that just like the world we inhabit every day, there are people online who aren't very nice—but no one ever claimed that an online service was a piece of heaven on earth. Sorry to say it, but the same kind of people you meet every day in the physical world are the people you'll meet online. You'll just be able to meet a lot more of them a lot more quickly. That's certainly one advantage of the virtual world over the physical one. And one of the ways of meeting a lot of people is to enter a chat room. These regulars are your best protection against unscrupulous individuals. This is especially true in the rooms that deal with arcane sexual topics like Dominance and Submission (D/S), where the possibility of abuse can be more real.

When you first cruise the online service of your choice, check out the rooms you think you'd like to frequent. Be cordial and polite, but also make note of the people who are in those rooms on a regular basis. Observe these regulars and get to know them. They know what's up and are most interested in keeping their rooms intact and free from minors and other disruptive people. And, who knows, one of those regulars may be the woman of your dreams.

Chatting in Private Rooms

In addition to public rooms, most services allow you to create *private rooms* that require a *key* to enter. Having the key means knowing a password or just the name of the room. You can create a private room by following the instructions of your online service and only giving the key to the people you want to enter, or you can be invited into a private room when someone else gives you the key. Private rooms can contain many people who just wish to deny access to the general public. For example, I was once involved in a public chat room that held a private meeting once a week to discuss room policies and to initiate worthy *newbies* (newcomers) into the inner circle. Many public rooms have this private-room component, and you know you've been accepted when you're invited into the private discussion.

Most often, private rooms are used by men and women to have private, and sometimes intimate, conversations. You'd certainly create a private room if you wanted to engage a woman in mutually agreed-upon cybersex. But private rooms are not used for sexual purposes alone. In services that have chat rooms, instant messaging systems, and a way to locate a person anywhere on the service, you can get really inundated with conversations. Sometimes you just want to talk to someone exclusively; shut off that instant messaging capability and have a nice private chat with that woman you want to know more about.

Chatting Using an Instant Messaging System

For services that have this capability, an *instant message* allows you to talk privately to anyone online just by knowing that person's name. Personally, I find this method of communicating the best. Chat rooms can be very confusing and diverse and it's sometimes difficult to attract a woman's attention. As I mentioned, chat rooms are great for finding out who the regulars are and what the people in that room are discussing. You may meet a woman in a public chat room, but you'll need to take the conversation to a private level to have a serious discussion. A private message has the advantage of being difficult to ignore, is conversational, and, unlike inviting a woman you just met into a private room, doesn't have sexual connotations. (Because of those connotations, it's not necessarily a successful strategy to invite a woman you just met into a private room.)

You also can hold private conversations with a number of women at the same time, without anyone knowing. Unless, of course, it takes you too long to answer, then it becomes obvious that you're talking to more than one person. This is a great time saver in your search for that particular woman. And it sure isn't something you can do in your local physical-world hot spot. I've had many successful conversations with women using the private message system.

Chatting on the World Wide Web

A new way to meet a woman is now emerging. It's live chat via Internet's World Wide Web facility. Previously, the World Wide Web was a great place to find information, but now, entrepreneurs have found a way to use the available bandwidth to engage in live chat. Right now, chatting on the World Wide Web is a bit cumbersome but, like everything about the Internet, it has great potential. Since Web Sites are run by companies and organizations with a specific geographic location, a World Wide Web chat site will most likely attract people who live in that area, so this could be the place of the future.

Chatting is chatting, whether it be on a small BBS, a large commercial service, or the Internet. We'll chat a lot more about chatting and how to make it work for you throughout the course of this book.

But there are so many other ways to meet a woman online, it's worth taking a look at them before we go back to chat. You may find one or more of these options worth a try, alone or combined with another.

Public Message Boards

A *public message board* is a system where people *post* (write an e-mail letter) messages about a particular topic of interest. Like a chat room, a public message board has a well-defined topic ranging from the mundane to the arcane and from the spiritual to the sexual. Public message boards may have different names, depending on the service you subscribe to, but for the sake of convenience, I'll use just two names: *forums* and *Usenet Groups*.

Forums

Forums are public boards that are specific to the service you subscribe to and can be read by any other member of that service. If you subscribe to a service with 100 members, 100 people will be able to read your post. If you subscribe to a service with five million members, any one of them can read your post. You can access these boards by going to the area of your service that contains them and either downloading them or reading them online.

Usenet Groups

Usenet Groups are specific to the Internet. There are more Usenet Groups on the Internet than you could read in five lifetimes, and they just keep growing in number and variety of topics. Some are extremely active, with hundreds of posts per day, and others have just a few. You can obtain a list of these groups from your Internet Service Provider.

13

Since approximately 30 million people troll the highways and by-ways of the Internet, these groups can be extremely public. In addition, most online services offer their members Internet access, so that adds a few million more people.

You access a Usenet Group by subscribing. Most services have made this a really simple point-and-click process. There is technically no limit to how many Usenet Groups you can subscribe to, but, unless you have a lot of time to read thousands of letters a day, it's best to choose these groups wisely. Once you subscribe, you'll be able to read what people say about that group's particular topic and add your thoughts to the general discussion, either to the group as a whole or by responding to a particular post, called "following a thread." The exact method of doing that may vary slightly from service to service, but it's pretty simple to figure out.

Another way to find out what's happening on a Usenet Group, without subscribing and getting inundated with a zillion letters, is by using one of the *search engines* available on the World Wide Web. These search engines allow you to search across multiple Usenet Groups for a key word or phrase. Let's say, for example, you want to find what people are saying about "gastroenteritis" (admittedly not a very romantic term). Go to one of these search engines, type the term, tell it to search Usenet Groups, and a list of letters (from a certain date) from every news group that search engine tracks will appear. You can read and respond to the letters right from the generated list. Using a search engine to investigate Usenet Groups is also a good way to find out if you want to subscribe to any of them.

Using Public Message Boards to Find a Woman

Except those boards that are specifically designed for meeting people, you will be expected to confine your posts to the topic of the message board. That is board etiquette. To do otherwise may get you *flamed*, that is, your mail box will be stuffed with hundreds and hundreds of nasty e-mail letters. Believe me, no one wants to be the object of a flame. Still, boards do bring together people with common interests, and anywhere people with similar tastes congregate can be a place to find a member of the opposite sex.

Like chat rooms, boards contain regulars, people who post consistently with intelligent things to say. As you become a regular, you may find that a particular lady is responding to your thread regularly. You may develop a rapport with her through the regular exchange of posts to the board. Since a post, in the vast majority of cases, contains that person's e-mail address, there's nothing in the world stopping you from sending her a private e-mail saying how much you enjoy reading her posts, and, through that, beginning a direct correspondence. It's possible that a woman may send you a direct e-mail saying how much she enjoys *your* posts. And, from that, a one-to-one relationship may develop.

Searching Membership Directories

Many services have membership directories in which you can list your-self, your interests, and other exciting facts you want other members to know about you. In some services, once you create a profile, you are automatically listed, so if you don't want to be listed, don't create one (creating an attractive profile is discussed in the next chapter). Since women who choose to list themselves already want you to know who they are, they would not be surprised or put off by finding a nice letter in their e-mail box introducing yourself.

In services that have a membership directory, you can find women who have similar interests or live near you by doing a keyword search. So, inputting the words:

```
Female AND Single AND Hiking AND MyTown
```

will give you a list of all single women in your town that enjoy hiking. The spelling of the keyword has to be exact, so if you type "New York," you won't get those who spelled it "NY." You may have to try different combinations of words and/or abbreviations to get a completely accurate list.

Once you have the list, you can peruse each one and see what other interests they may share with you; some may list a birthdate or age, and many are just plain interesting. Perhaps one or more of these women will strike your fancy and you may choose to send them e-mail, telling them that you found them in a search, that you also enjoy hiking, and you live in the same town.

You probably won't get responses to all of your e-mail, and some of them will respond with, "Hey, why don't you just *take* a hike," but you may get a very pleasant response from one or two and an opportunity to build from there. And I'm sure you have more interests than hiking; you can do any number of keyword searches, any one of which will have the possibility of finding the woman of your dreams.

If your service has a membership directory, that can also play an important role in your success at live chat. Why? Because before you approach a woman, you can check her profile and find out what she says about herself. When I'm on a service that has this capability, I never speak to a woman without a profile. My first approach to a woman is always to compliment what she says about herself; without a profile, I'm in the dark. Let's face it: People like to hear compliments. Why make it difficult when you can make it easy? Enough women have profiles on these services that you can ignore those without.

Personal Advertising the Cyberspace Way

This is the cyber-age, and personal advertising, the way it's done in the personals section of your newspaper, can be done in cyberspace—but with a major interactive difference. On the World Wide Web, for example, many pages are devoted to women seeking men and men seeking women. Match.com at World Wide Web address http://www.match.com, for example, has been a highly successful way to meet a member of the opposite sex. They have over 90,000 registered members worldwide and claim to be responsible for quite a few successful marriages.

A service like Match.com, which does have a small monthly fee, not only allows its members to search for love but also gives them the ability to send e-mail to each other without divulging their e-mail names until they're ready to. This ability to send anonymous e-mail has proven successful, because women tend to be a bit more cautious about relating personal information than men. Consequently, Match.com has a high percentage of female members.

But on any of these personal ads areas, you'll be able to find women from all over the world. And because these pages are databases, you can input search terms to quickly narrow a search. So, if you're looking for a 5'4" blonde from Russia, you'll be able to narrow your search accordingly. Many pages also contain pictures of the women who are seeking men, as well as a general description and their interests. In addition, some women link their personal home page to their ad, so you can click on that and find out significantly more about them. When you find someone you want to contact, all you need to do is click on the e-mail address and write them a letter. That's all there is to it.

Of course, you can place your own ad on one of these World Wide Web sites, or in the many personal sections available on the commercial online services. In some instances, you'll be able to link a personal home page you've created so that anyone interested can find out more about you than you can place in the ad. You may also be able to attach a photo of yourself.

Looking through the Photo Gallery

There are thousands and thousands and *thousands* of photos online. All of the major commercial online services have a photo gallery where members can place photos of themselves or works of art they've created for the enjoyment of other members. You can view these photos online, or download them for later viewing offline. Some services provide a keyword-searchable database for the photo gallery so you can use it the same way I described searchng the membership directory.

Not all of the women who put their photos in the gallery are looking for men. Some just want their online friends to know what they look like; some just like being seen. But, if you see someone you like, there's no reason why you can't just send an e-mail and introduce yourself.

Playing Games

For those of you who get a kick out of playing casino games, chess, backgammon, checkers, trivia, or any of a number of other games, you will find ample locations on the major online services and the Internet, which has all the games just mentioned as well as interactive role playing games variously called MUDs (Multi-User Dungeon), MUSHes (Multi-User Shared Hallucination), and MOOs (MUD Object-Oriented).

The problem with most gaming areas is that, while they are interactive and provide opportunities to meet people, you usually have no control over who your opponent is. Most of them operate on a first-come, first-serve basis. Games provide entertainment and diversion, but I don't recommend the gaming areas of online services or the Internet as the prime location for finding a mate.

Face to Face (F2F) Get-Togethers

One distinct advantage local BBSs have over the commercial online services and ISPs is their propensity for inviting members to get together *real-time* (RT) and meet *f2f*. Since most BBSs have just a few hundred members and most of whom live in the area where the BBS is located, these meetings are easily organized. And since they are always held in a public place, under the auspices of the BBS management, any fears a woman may have about meeting that anonymous person she has been corresponding with are usually minimal.

If you become a member of a BBS, you should definitely take advantage of these RT meetings. At the very least, you'll have the BBS in common with the other people there, and who knows—perhaps you and the woman you seem to have hit it off with online will end up sitting at a nice cozy table in the corner for a more private chat.

While BBSs provide a more organized meeting environment, they're not the only places where RT get-togethers occur. Today's online environment, as chaotic as it sometimes appears to a newcomer, is actually a fairly well-organized community, with citizens who have been online for years. As I mentioned previously, the chat rooms of the commercial online services and the IRC, as well as forums, have themes and people interested in that theme who congregate in those places. After a while, a community of regulars forms, leaders emerge, and an organization develops.

Often the people who share the particular interest of the chat room or forum plan get-togethers at a restaurant, a club, a trade show of interest to the group, or in someone's private residence. One of the benefits, then, of becoming a regular in this organically grown community is the chance to be invited to one of these group events. So, why not invite that lady you've been chatting with to meet you f2f at one of these informal gatherings and see what develops? Of course, unlike get-togethers at the local BBS, these meetings may involve considerable travel and expense.

A Home Page of Your Own

Creating a *home page*, that is, a file that can be accessed through the World Wide Web, is not in itself a proactive means of finding a woman,

18

but it can be a great marketing tool to give people a good thumbnail sketch of who you are. As in any situation where you want to meet people, what you put in a Web page should show you at your best. Be witty without being overbearing, intelligent without being lofty, and show your interests and be friendly without being patronizing.

Creating a personal home page doesn't require the technical knowledge it once did. Many online services have simple point-and-click facilities that allow you to create a page in very short order. In addition, page-creation programs are available, both commercially and for free on the Internet.

3 Defining your Goals

Now that you have some idea of where to meet women online, the next question is, who do you want to meet? In a world as diverse as the online one, where there are so many possibilities, the question of who you want to meet is most easily answered by defining what you are looking for.

In the physical world, the one we inhabit every day, there are really just three choices you're looking for: a permanent relationship, a date (with one or more women, with or without the thought of a permanent relationship), or an affair. We all know that life is a little tricky, and sometimes we start out with one goal in mind and end up with a very different result, but, in general, if you want a permanent relationship, you won't flirt with or try to date married or otherwise spoken-for women. That would be a waste of time and energy, not to mention possibly dangerous. On the other hand, if you're just looking to have an affair, your playing field may be somewhat broader. The point is, you make choices based on your goal.

The online world is exactly the same as the RT one: You have to make choices based on your goal. However, you'll have to consider another set of choices available in the online world. Those choices have to do with the environment you'll operate in. The online world not only adds a veneer to the physical world but, in a very real sense, is its own reality. So, you have to multiply the possibilities of the physical world by two, because whatever you can do in the physical you can also do in the cyber. This may sound strange to you now, if you haven't done it, but it

21

is possible to have a cyber relationship, engage in cyber dating, or have a cyber affair in addition to using the online environment to find an RT relationship, engage in RT dating, and look for an RT affair.

That's why it's a good idea to know what you want before you go after it.

Some Definitions

Before we start this process, let's first define some of the terms I'll be using in this book.

Virtual Relationship: All relationships on the online environment start as virtual, but I'll use this term strictly to define a relationship that has no possibility of ever translating itself into the physical world.

Why do people engage in virtual relationships? Well, they are people who, for a variety of reasons, cannot pursue a physical relationship. They may be married, they may have some physical disability that prevents them from having a physical relationship, or they may be incredibly shy in person. They are not necessarily ugly or unlovable people; their circumstances just prevent them from having any other kind of relationship, and many find it quite satisfying.

A virtual relationship is not an unreal relationship. There is no such thing as an unreal relationship; relationships are never unreal. Just because it remains online does not mean there is no level of commitment. Emotions can grow and be demonstrated, dates can be made and kept, jealousy can exist. In short, any emotion that you can exhibit in the RT world can exist in the virtual one—everything but actual physical contact.

Potential Relationship: A potential relationship has the possibility of becoming an RT relationship. It's sometimes not easy to distinguish between a virtual relationship and a potential one, especially in the early stages. What determines the difference is the willingness of both partners to progress into the other stages: the telephone stage and the meeting stage. You'll learn how to distinguish between a virtual and a potential relationship in this book.

Online Relationship: A generic term, encompassing both virtual and potential relationships.

Real Time (RT) Relationship: A relationship that started online and has successfully translated itself into the physical world. Do not get confused by the "real" in "real time." A distinction is often made between online and real relationships, as though online relationships are somehow unreal. That is certainly not the case. An online relationship, as you will discover in the course of this book, can be every bit as "real" as a real relationship.

The Four Stages...

Every relationship that becomes RT goes through four stages of development. These are:

- ◉ The virtual stage
- ◉ The potential stage
- ◉ The voice (telephone) stage
- ◉ The real time stage

...and the Three Courtships

As you can see, the four stages involve three very definite transitions as you move from the online environment to hearing the other person's voice to seeing that person in real time. One of the most exciting facets of pursuing a relationship with a woman in this manner is get to know her for the first time *three* times: once online, once on the telephone, and once in person. No other kind of relationship allows for so much romance and courtship on so many different levels.

Do I Want a Virtual or a Potential Relationship?

Although the main focus of this book is about how to progress from a potential relationship to an RT relationship, you can also use the same techniques and suggestions to develop a virtual relationship. In fact, you can even more liberally apply the criteria I discuss if what you want is a virtual relationship. So, it is a legitimate question and let's start by asking if what you want is something virtual or something with potential. Whether you want something virtual or something with potential depends on your own personal circumstances. If you've been out of the dating scene for a while, either by choice or by marriage, something

23

virtual may be a great way to have a relationship without dealing with someone face-to-face. It's also a great way to get back into the dating scene, since the fear of being rejected online is considerably milder than it is in the RT world. Plus, there are literally thousands of women online at any given time, whereas in a club, if you strike out once, that could be your evening. In addition, you can have a virtual relationship with a woman who lives practically anywhere, whereas looking for an RT relationship may restrict your search to a closer proximity for economic reasons.

We'll take a closer look at the emotional aspects of online relationships in Chapter 6, so you may want to read that one before making a firm decision. For now, keep in mind that virtual relationships, whether they're one-to-one, multiple-dating types, or affairs, can have emotional aspects, so they can be satisfying, annoying, or even heartbreaking. I didn't say there's no baggage to a virtual relationship, just that there's no face-to-face baggage.

Why Can't I Have Both?

You can! There is no online code of ethics that says you cannot pursue both virtual and potential relationships at the same time. And there's no doubt that for a while, you'll probably do just that. Just keep in mind that all relationships consume time and energy, and there's no point in pursuing a virtual relationship at the expense of a potential one. Keep in mind too that feelings develop even in virtual relationships, and when it comes time to tell your virtual partner that you've met someone, it may not be as easy as you think.

Perhaps you don't want a virtual relationship at all. That's great—you've come to the right place. That's what this book is all about! If your main aim is finding an RT relationship from your cyber advances, you'll want to consider the following questions. You may come up with additional questions to ask yourself, depending on your individual RT circumstances.

How Serious Am I about Finding a Woman Online?

As in any endeavor, success is usually a product of commitment. Finding a woman via an online service does involve an investment of time and energy. There is not only the time involved in seeking and talking

24

to someone online; there is also the time involved in writing e-mail on a regular basis. If you end up having more than one online relationship, the time involved in maintaining them can be considerable. Let's face it: It takes a lot longer to write a letter than it does to say the same thing. I know people who spend just about all of their time writing and answering e-mail.

So before you get started, keep in mind that searching for a woman via an online service may take time away from other pursuits.

What Are My Resources?

Depending on the service or services you subscribe to, online time can be costly. Most of the major commercial services, for example, give you a limited number of hours per month as part of your monthly membership fee and then charge by the hour after that. Some even have additional charges for the privilege of chatting. Since it's so simple to just sit in your easy chair and sign on, you may not be fully aware of the cost until you get your credit-card statement—and the amount can knock you right out of that easy chair. It's a good idea to decide beforehand how much money you want to spend—and stick to it. (As of this writing, America Online has announced a new flat-rate monthly fee for unlimited use. Will CompuServe, Prodigy, and other services that charge by the hour follow AOL's lead to stay competitive? You bet! So, online service fees may become a minimal factor in your search.)

When it comes time to make that first phone call to someone you met online but haven't met f2f, you'll have to deal with another cost factor. Long-distance relationships can get costly. Telephone charges mount up rapidly. And as easy as it is to sign on to a service, it's even easier to pick up the phone and dial. As the man, you may still be expected to pay these bills. Yes, that's the way it is, guys. The online environment may be a liberated one but it's not that liberated, and even if you're independently wealthy, you may not be prepared to spend a couple-thousand dollars a month on telephone charges for a woman you haven't even met.

Once again, it's best to figure out your resources beforehand, in the cool, rational light of reason, and stick to it even after your emotions become involved. Even when you enjoy talking for hours on the telephone, it's still best to come to an agreement with her about dividing your time among the telephone, in which you are most likely paying; live online time, where you both pay an equal amount; and e-mail, where you can say an awful lot for pennies.

Now, having said all that, we all know that courtship can be expensive, and even in the RT world we can sure end up spending a lot more on the lady of our dreams than we originally planned. So, you know that figure you just decided you won't go over? Add a few dollars—just to be on the safe side.

Technology has made it possible to cut long-distance phone bills down to local-call size. With the right hardware and software, you can now make a telephone call to anyone, anywhere in the world via the Internet for the price of connecting to the Internet (usually a local call, plus connect-time charges, if any). And, with some additional hardware and software, you can turn that voice-only call into a video conference call. What more can you ask for?

Do I Want to Find Someone Close-By or Far Away?

Distance or proximity: That is one troubling question when meeting your mate online that really doesn't enter into RT situations. In the online world there are always more people who live further away from you than live in your immediate area, even if you live in a large metropolitan area. This is especially true with the commercial online services and most definitely with the Internet. So, in the online world, your chances of meeting someone who lives a great distance from you are quite high.

Meeting someone who lives far away isn't necessarily a bad thing, and it's certainly not a hopeless situation. In fact, one of the beautiful things about meeting a woman online is the fact that you are not constrained by geographic boundaries; it's just as easy to meet someone on the other side of the country—or the world—as it is to meet someone on the other side of town. If you do meet someone who lives far away, take heart from the fact that we live in a highly mobile society in which about seven percent of the entire population moves each year. You can also take heart that thousands of people have already met online, and many move to be with the one they fell in love with. Many of these people have found happiness, so it *is* possible.

What you have to think about when making this decision is future costs involved in maintaining a long-distance relationship. At some point, if things go well online, you'll want to speak to that person over the phone and, later on, you'll want to have a f2f meeting. These costs can be considerable—in fact, they can be astronomical. I've known people who spent $1,000 per month and more in long distance (Know them? I am one!), not to mention airline fares. Needless to say, meeting a woman from another country is even more costly. Nonetheless, many men prefer to meet a woman who is not from their geographical area (perhaps they are from an urban area and are looking for a more rural-type woman) and accept these costs as the price of finding the right woman.

The other obvious disincentive to meeting a woman who lives a great distance away is in the difficulty of actualizing the online relationship in the RT world if it really does work out. There are the questions of who moves, who pays for the move, who pays for the move back if things don't work out.... These can be complicated and difficult questions to answer. And, unfortunately, sometimes love just isn't enough and a beautiful online relationship turns to dust amidst the stress and chaos of answering and sorting out these questions.

The obvious solution is to give up on the idea of finding a woman who lives far away, but that's a defeatist attitude and, quite honestly, with that attitude you'll never find a woman near or far, online or off. No, that's certainly not the answer. The answer, of course, is to decide what you're looking for in a woman and be prepared to go after her, regardless of the distance involved. You now know that this may be costly, so prepare for it.

If you really want to find a woman who lives in your area, there are ways of increasing your chances. One is to stick to the local BBSs. The other is to sign up with the commercial online services but sign on to them at the hours most conducive to meeting women from your area, or at least your part of the country. For example, if you're from the East Coast, you'll increase your chances of meeting someone from your geographic area if you sign on by 8 p.m., when it's earlier in other parts of the country. Just like any hot spot in the physical world, online services have prime-time hours. Because of the local time differences, prime time for your area will always be different than prime time for other areas.

Do I Want Something Serious or Something Light?

Are you looking for that perfect someone, with whom you can share every thought and feeling for the rest of your life? Well, some of us are, and if you're one of them, that's great. Or are you looking for a fling? If you are, that's great, too.

27

In the online world you can meet literally hundreds of people in a single night, some of whom will undoubtedly have the same objective as you. So you won't waste your time convincing someone who just wants to have a fling that she really needs to have a relationship with you because you're perfect for each other.

That's certainly one of the great aspects of doing all this online—there's no need to play the games you may have become accustomed to in your RT-world dating. You can be more direct about your intentions, while maintaining proper discretion, than you can in the RT world. If you're looking for that afternoon tête-à-tête, there's someone online who's looking for the same thing. And, you'll find, they will be just as direct as you.

Creating Your Online Personality

In the RT world, what people see first is your appearance—the way you dress, your mannerisms—and that, to a large extent, forms that all-important first impression. In the online world, where appearance is non-existent, that first impression is created through your screen name and, where available, the information you place in your profile. Let's take a look at these two crucial aspects of online life.

What's in a Name?

You would never introduce yourself as The Writer, or Body Surfer, or Out For Fun, or More Dominant in the RT world. But in the virtual world, real names are boring, and secondary. In the virtual world, the important thing is to present an evocative image of yourself through the use of words.

The first thing a woman sees of you is the pseudonym you give yourself. These pseudonyms are variously called *e-mail names*, *screen names*, *handles*, or *nicknames*. Whatever you call them, they should, in a few letters or words, give a woman some idea of who you are—and spark some interest. Most services give you the opportunity to create an interesting name when you sign on with them, or allow you to do it at a later time. Spending a little time designing a name that feels right to you and projects the image you want is worth the effort.

My personal preference is to pick a name from ancient mythology that isn't commonly known. I do this because 1) I'm looking for a woman who has broad-based knowledge,

2) Such names are better attention grabbers and conversation starters, and 3) Such names are usually not known to minors. So, when I enter a room and some woman says:

```
Everybody watch your step, the Egyptian God of the Dead
has just entered the room.
```

I already know quite a bit about that person, even before I begin speaking to her.

Find out how the service assigns names before you sign up. If you're signing up with a service that allows you only one name, do your research before signing up. Since e-mail names have to be unique to any given service, the name you choose may already be taken. Have a couple back-ups handy just in case that happens. If you plan on using your e-mail name for letters to Mom and business associates, it's probably not a good idea to call yourself IAmSlave4U.

Many Internet service providers allow you to have a second e-mail name for a small additional monthly fee. However, if you're dealing with an ISP, the chances are you'll be spending most of your cruising time on International Relay Chat. Before entering the IRC you will have an opportunity to create a name, but there's no guarantee that the name won't be taken by someone else. Nor are there any guarantees that a name you use one day will not be taken by someone else the next, so it's very difficult to create a consistent online persona on IRC. Your best bet is to be as creative as possible. Of course, someone may very well steal that creative name.

CompuServe gives you a number to use as your e-mail name but allows you to create a handle before entering its chat area. CompuServe gives you the option of having a reserved handle for an additional charge. America Online allows a user to create up to five screen names, each of which you can also use to send and receive e-mail. When you first sign up, AOL suggests a name based on your first and last names. You can accept this name or choose another. Personally, I would accept the name AOL assigns and then create a more interesting name or names for use in the chat areas. The reason? You can't delete the first screen name, but you can create and delete the other names at will. Prodigy separates your e-mail name from the name you give yourself in the chat area and allows you to change that name once a day.

Whichever service you use and however many names that service allows you to create, using a consistent name helps you get known to others in the online community and helps you to get to know others. Your chances of finding a woman who is "real" and dependable are greatly increased when you yourself are real and dependable.

Creating a Profile

Once you have a screen name you like, it's time to create a profile. Here again, services differ in your ability to create a profile, but, if you are using one that gives you that ability, it's a good idea to create one. In fact, on those services, some women won't even talk to you if you don't have a profile.

The object of creating a profile, like a good screen name, is to let that woman whom you contact, or who contacts you, know something about you. The more interesting and inviting you make it, the more inclined a woman will be to contact you or keep talking to you. A well-written profile also helps eliminate those people who do not share your particular interests, and gives people who do a handy reference point to start a conversation. You can also see by your conversation with a woman whether she's made the effort of checking your profile.

The object of a profile is not to be disgusting and turn everyone off, although that does seem to be the object of plenty of profiles I've read through the years. One might wonder what the people behind those profiles are thinking.

In a profile, you can also state the things you will not do. Many people say "No cyber (sex); no phone (sex)" to automatically eliminate those people who are only interested in a sexual encounter. Since, you'll find, those who are only interested in sex won't prove to be serious contenders as a potential mate, it does little harm, and possibly a lot of good, to eliminate them right from the beginning.

When creating a profile, it's a good idea to put into it what you plan to get out of your online experience. It's really most important to sound intelligent and to put some thought behind it. It's not necessary to be directly sexual. Let's face it, most women think all we're after is sex anyway, so it's not necessary to put any direct references to sex or anatomy into your profile. For most women, words like "really slung" or "best lay in town" are turn-offs. It's quite all right to use words that are sensual, provocative, and romantic, and show a caring and thoughtful person.

Before you create a profile, look at other people's profiles and get some ideas. There are many interesting and provocative profiles to look at. If something catches your eye, it's okay to use something similar. After all, imitation is the sincerest form of flattery.

Scan Thyself

How would you like to have your picture available to millions of women via the World Wide Web or the photo library of one of the major online services? You can, and it's very easy to do. All you need is to have your photo scanned into a computer as a graphic and upload it. Most large photocopy shops will scan your photos at a reasonable cost, and all the major online services offer their members free scanning and uploading. You don't have to be a technocrat to have your photo scanned.

As already noted, thousands upon thousands of people are doing it. It can be a great source of information for you in your search, but it can also be a great place for a woman to find you as well. If you do upload your photo into your service's photo gallery, be sure to mention its location in your profile so that women can take a look at you.

Even if you don't upload your photo for public consumption, it's still a good idea to get a good recent photo (or a few of them) scanned. At some point in your online relationship, the time will come when you will want to know what that person you've been communicating with looks like, and she'll want to know what you look like. Having the photos available on your hard drive will make the process a lot smoother and, if it comes early in your relationship, before you even speak on the phone, it avoids the necessity of asking for her mailing address.

Facilitating RT Communication

One major concern in dealing with people online is exchanging RT telephone numbers and mailing addresses. As I mentioned above, having a scanned photo of yourself that you can e-mail to a potential mate facilitates the exchange of critical information while eliminating the need to exchange addresses. Thus, the exchange can be made much earlier in the course of a relationship, sometimes within the first hour of speaking to a person online, than might otherwise be the case.

There are other things you may want to consider doing that will make the exchange of information more feasible at an earlier date, while still taking prudent precautions to maintain your anonymity. If you are

31

really serious about finding a mate online and interested in moving to RT quickly, one of the must-haves is a post office box. The post office box has long been an effective technique used by people who respond to ads in the personals. While it is possible to get the name behind the post office box from the post office, this fact is not generally known (until now?) and is not usually utilized. So, establishing a post office box is a fairly safe way to facilitate communication and to exchange photos.

It might also be mentioned that having a post office box helps quicken the development of trust since, while it's not your home address, it does verify to the woman you are talking to that you live in the area you claim. It is highly unlikely for you to live in New York and maintain a post office box in Virginia.

I've also met many men online who maintain 800 numbers, which they seem to give to women fairly liberally. All the major long distance carriers now have the capability of offering personal 800 (or the new 888) numbers to their customers, usually at a very reasonable monthly cost. However, don't forget that you have to pay for all the calls you receive and charges can be as high as $25 per hour. I know of one gentleman who did this and, in a very short time, had eight women calling him regularly. He can afford the calls, but if you can't, this is not an option for you.

A somewhat less expensive alternative is to have another phone line installed that you can use just for people you meet online. The fact of the matter is, if you spend considerable time online, it's probably a good idea to have a second line installed just for use as a data line. Then if you ever get to a point where you don't want to speak to those online people, you can have your number changed, without the hassle of having to tell friends, family, and creditors that they have to now call you on a different number. Make sure this number is unlisted and, if possible in your area, that Caller ID service is blocked or buy a Caller-ID blocker. (Of course, you never have to worry about Caller ID when calling long distance.)

And, finally, the least-expensive method is to use distinctive ringing if it's available in your area. Distinctive ringing gives you a second number on your already installed telephone line that, appropriately enough, has a different ring from your main phone number.

Let's Sign on— And cruise

④

On any given night there are thousands of people in chat rooms on the commercial online services or the IRC. America Online, for example, claims to have from 400,000 to 500,000 people online every Saturday night. And from what I've seen, most of them are in the chat rooms. What are these people doing? Let's rev up that computer and find out. First, double click on that attractive icon representing your online service, sit back, and wait while your modem transports you into a different world. That squeaking and squawking coming from your modem that sounds like your brakes need an adjustment indicate you are arriving at your destination. You've already traveled quite a distance and you haven't even left the comfort of your own home. With just a few more mouse clicks you'll be cruising into a space that is unlike any local hot spot anywhere on the face of the earth.

Whether you've set your computer to teleport you to the Internet's International Relay Chat, America Online or Prodigy's chat rooms, CompuServe's CB Channels, any other major online service, or one of the thousands of BBSs around the country—wherever people gather for live chat—you'll find hundreds, even thousands of areas, filled with people of every type and description. They're doing just about anything people can do: talking, flirting, engaging in lewd public displays, having intellectual conversations, arguing, discussing the weather, or just sitting quietly and watching what other people are doing. It's all there, anything and everything you can think of, and more.

There's so much here that, if you're a newbie (someone new to this environment), it can take a while to get your bearings. Even the experts take some time deciding which of their favorite places they'd like to go. That's OK; take you're time, you're just exploring. First, look around and figure out where you are.

If your destination is America Online, your first stop is a chat room called variously The Lobby, Laura's Love Lounge, Jake LaMotta, or whatever name AOL decides to use for your foray into the chat area. You can stay in that room or go to any one of the hundreds of chat rooms AOL has to offer. IRC places you into what I call a cybervoid, where you're surrounded by cybersilence. From that point, you'll have to get a list of rooms and enter one before you can engage in public chat. CompuServe and Prodigy also place you in some sort of cybervoid.

Personally, I like the idea of being thrown into the middle of the action and working my way around from there, but that's a matter of taste. No matter where you go, you'll be able to get a list of rooms, the people in those rooms, and, if available, some information on the people who have created profiles for themselves. You'll also be able to talk privately to another person if you know they're there.

Scoping Out Cyberchat Space

Take a few moments to get your bearings and find out what's out there. If you find yourself in an AOL chat room, say hello to the other people in the room. Although this first stop is mainly a transitory place used as a jumping-off point to other rooms, it never hurts to be polite. Perhaps there'll be some interesting conversation in the lounge. If not, you can get a list of the other rooms and see who's in each, check profiles of those screen names that seem interesting, and talk privately to anyone in any other room or anyone signed on to AOL.

You can do something similar in IRC and CompuServe but, because neither places you in a chat room initially, you cannot participate in room chat until you actually enter a room. Prodigy gives you the ability to select a destination before you sign on, so you can select "chat" and you'll be placed at the entrance to their chat facility. But you still have to click a mouse button or two before you can participate.

You may find room chat quite confusing at first. Words, simulated actions, direct and indirect sexual comments, and role-playing scroll by, sometimes at dizzying speeds. On a CompuServe channel, where you

34

can have over a hundred people in one room, 40 lines of text from five different conversations may separate your response to a comment made just seconds before. Whew! Who said what to whom? There are sometimes so many conversations going on it's difficult to know.

It's like walking into a large RT party. As you look at the throngs of people before you, you'll notice that some people are alone but most are broken up into various groups. You'll hear the general buzz of people laughing and speaking but, unless you're standing next to a group, you won't be able to make hear any of the conversation. As you survey the room, perhaps you'll see a woman standing alone you'd like to speak to and, after verifying that she is, in fact, alone, you'll casually make your way in her direction. Perhaps you'll try to establish eye contact and see if it is returned before you actually speak to her.

A chat room is similar to entering a large RT party, with a number of essential differences. You'll be able to "hear" all of the public conversations going on. That's why it's sometimes difficult to pick up the thread of an individual conversation. You won't be able to hear any private conversations going on, no matter how close you "stand" to someone else. You'll be able to engage in any number of public and private conversations simultaneously, although that number is limited by how fast you can think on your feet and how fast you can type. And, finally, you can bet that there's no such thing as a woman standing alone in the corner. Even if you don't see her chatting in the room, you can be assured she's having a number of private conversations.

Plunging into Chat

The best way to find out what's happening in a chat room is to just plunge right in. Press **Join, Go, Tune,** or do a **/JOIN #roomname**, whatever your particular service requires you to do, and step into a chat room. Don't forget to say hello when you enter.

The following screen shows an example of a conversation you might find in a chat room. For this example I've more or less used America Online as a prototype. Take a look at it. Imagine sitting in front of your computer with words scrolling quickly up the screen in front of you. Better yet, after you take a look at it here, sign on to your favorite service and take a look at the live version. If you haven't been in your service's chat area before, now is a good time to do it. But don't get lost in cyberspace and forget to come back to the book. We're just at the threshold of the important stuff. BTW (by the way), you are WordSmithl.

35

OnlineHost:	*** You are in "Sensual Melange" ***
JetFighter:	poor Beth had her hands full yesterday.
WhizKid:	good evening everyone, just passing through!
Shellbeee:	Hey, poutygirl, what'd ya wearing tonite?
LordDice:	JF, why if i may ask?
PassionFlr:	Anyone would have her hands full with you, JF. <— personal experience. hehehehehehe
WordSmithI:	hello all
ChiefOne:	Anyone from Indiana in the room? 25/m
JetFighter:	......because she had to deal w/me on the phone last night! LOL
Poutygirl:	<—wearing micro mini neon pink skater skirt, soft angora cropped top (belly button shows) and cute black baby jane patent leather high heels with white, lacy bobby socks.
StackOTble:	mondays suck after a good weekend
JetFighter:	thanks for the vote of confidence
PassionFlr:	{{{{{{{{{{{{{{{WORD}}}}}}}}}}}}}}}}
RichGirl:	Hey, 23/f/small town, IN
MyBeemie:	What do you do, stack?
PassionFlr:	ah, just funnin ya :)
Shellbeee:	Hoosier Girl
StackOTble:	poutys hot do you have long longs?
WordSmithI:	Hey, passion.
MyBeemie:	RiiiiichGiiiiirlllll!!!!!!!!!!!!!!!!!
StackOTble:	do or did?
MyBeemie:	::raises an eyebrow at pouty:::

```
RichGirl:       you bet
ChiefOne:       <- Indianapolis
Poutygirl:      very long. <- 5'11".
Shellbeee:      im in love
MyBeemie:       did.
RichGirl:       hey, beemie what's up??????????
StackOTble:     ur legggggggggs?
JJonesOU:       hi room
StackOTble:     weekend in Maui
RichGirl:       what'd ya do, chief?
Just4Kicks:     hello, new folks
MyBeemie:       coooooool beats working any day
Poutygirl:      lol, stack. My height.
MyBeemie:       nuttin honey
ChiefOne:       strategic materials manager
Just4Kicks:     and rich too. My kinda girl.
WhizKid:        didn't know there were any strategic
                materials in Indiana
RichGirl:       need a stable hand to groom the horses.
                pay minimum wage and a cot above the
                stables
MyBeemie:       Take a bow pouty
Just4Kicks:     emailing resume
Poutygirl:      oooooh, a cute lil' curtsy?
```

Chat Room Dynamics

Did you follow all that? If you didn't, that's OK. You walked into the middle of ongoing conversations, scene-playing, and role-playing activities. You can see some scene-playing in the actions of PoutyGirl. She's not actually wearing a micro-mini skirt as she types—and no one in the room really believes she is. She's creating a mood so that others can join in. She's play-acting by setting a scene. You will also find rooms with people involved in role-playing; they take on the personas of real or imaginary characters. You'll find whole groups of people who name themselves after *Star Trek* characters, for example.

It takes a couple of minutes to follow the threads of all the different activities. And it might take a while longer to get involved in one, or start your own. It was sure nice to have PassionFlr give you such a warm welcome, wasn't it? All those parentheses before and after WORD are meant to express warmth, like an embrace. Did you get the feeling that she was embracing you with those expressions? It's a nice feeling, isn't it? And it's something you can expect once you get to be known in a particular room. You'll form a bond with the people in the room and you'll be greeted warmly when you enter. And what could be better than having PassionFlr embrace you? You're a lucky guy.

If you're new to the room, your reception may not be that warm. You may get some polite hellos; or no response to your greeting at all. It's possible no one even said hello to you or responded to your hello. Don't be offended. Rooms can be cliquish and no one knows you yet, so people are not necessarily going to be that friendly. This is not as negative as it seems. Everybody in that room was once unknown to the others, as well, and had to work their way into the inner circle.

If you intend to become a regular in a room, regular visits and a demonstration that you know, or would like to know, about the topic will soon make you known, liked, and respected. Adult rooms that have regulars also provide a good check against some of the negative things that happen online that the media are so fond of covering (or uncovering). By becoming a regular in the chat area, you'll get to know the rooms, what type of people frequent them, and how people interact. You can be more certain that the people are who they say they are.

Many services allow you to change names any time you enter a chat room. If you like staying anonymous while you play online, you'll probably want to regularly change your screen name. However, it is far better to maintain a consistent screen name and become known to others. And to be new and also a man is not exactly the prescription to get noticed right off the bat. The other men in the room are not interested in you, unless, of course, you've entered a room in which men are interested in other men. And the women in the room are getting plenty of attention from the men in the room. The online environment, while attracting increasing numbers of women,

38

is still predominantly male. The women know this, and it's a rare but refreshing experience to find a woman who is willing to initiate a conversation with you when she's already inundated by any number of conversations with other people. Having an interesting screen name helps, but you can't count on that alone to get you noticed by any women. Even if a woman should show some interest, it's still be up to you to carry the ball from there. Remember there are far more men online than women.

As you can see, there are quite a few more people in the room than were talking. That's usually the case. Of the 25 people in the room there are 20 men and 5 women. (I'll get into distinguishing the men from the women below.) That's about right. Men outnumber women four to one on most online services, and that's about the ratio you'd expect to find in a chat room. No wonder so few women need to initiate chat.

But it's even more complicated than that, because the cyber walls that form a chat room are very thin indeed. In fact, they are non-existent, so not only do people in the chat room have access to other people in the same chat room but people from anywhere in the chat area can talk to other people anywhere in the chat area by using the private messaging system.

You can get an understanding of this by imagining an RT stadium that holds 200,000 people all looking to flirt, meet, and engage in erotic conversation, but out of those 200,000, 170,000 men are competing for the attention of 30,000 women. Now complicate that by the fact that the man sitting as far away from you as possible can talk to the woman you're sitting next to as easily as you can. You lose any advantage location would give you in the RT world.

Who's In This Chat Room?

To see what I mean, take a look at the following screen which shows the list of people in *Sensual Melange* as it may appear on your service (keep in mind that this list will constantly change as people enter and exit the room).

    AvatarX
    BigFish
    Bombardier
    ChiefOne
    CruisinGuy
    ImTheOne
    JetFighter
    JJonesOU
    Just4Kicks
    LadyOloff
    LadysGuy
    LordDice
    MackNYC
    MyBeemie
    PassionFlr
    Poutygirl
    RichGirl
    Shellbeee
    Shielder
    SinfulSir
    StackOTble
    WhizKid
    WordSmithI
    Zanathorpe
    ZestyyOne

39

But complicate that even further by the fact that you can speak to any number of women at the same time. So, let's say each man sends a message to 10 women. The ratio, in that case, becomes a lot greater than four to one; it becomes ten to one. Now don't turn off that computer just yet. We'll be looking at ways to change the odds in your favor. For now, just sit back, relax, and enjoy the conversation taking place in the room.

Getting Some Information

It's not too difficult to distinguish between the sexes when the people are talking, but what about the people who aren't? Can you tell the difference between the male names and the female names? Even if a screen name doesn't have a real name in it like Mack(NYC) or a distinguishing gender reference like Lady(Oloff), you can usually tell who is a man and who is a woman.

Take a look at ZestyyOne and Bombardier. Would you be willing to say that ZestyyOne is a woman and Bombardier a man? You'd be right if you did. But let's look at their profiles to be sure. Once again, we'll more or less use an America Online kind of profile, since the members on America Online put a lot of effort into their profiles and America Online gives them the space to do it. So, let's just click on the **Info** button and see what comes up:

```
Profile of ZestyyOne
Screen Name:        ZestyyOne
                    Member Name:     ZestyyOne
                    Location:  Northeast, USA
                    Birthdate: Yes
                    Sex: Female
                    Marital Status:  Single

Computers:          A drab gray one. Could anyone paint it
                    pink? :)

Hobbies:            Swimming; art; sensual, intelligent,
                    humorous, handsome men

Occupation:         Professional by day, ??? by night

Quote:              Live life to the fullest, but do so
                    honestly and ethically
```

40

```
Profile of Bombardier
Screen Name:        Bombardier
                    Member Name:    Michael
                    Location:  Salt Lake City
                    Birthdate: Old enough
                    Sex: Male
                    Marital Status:  Divorced
Computers:          PentiumPro - a screamin machine
Hobbies:            Flying, Skiing, Golf
Occupation:         Better than yours
Quote:              Been there, done that
```

Yep. ZestyyOne sure sounds like a woman to me, and Bombardier sounds like a man. Notice, too, the difference in the way the profiles are worded. Even if Zestyy didn't say she was a woman, her profile has a entirely different quality from Bombardier's. It's difficult to fake this stuff.

Do People Lie Online?

Can you really be sure people are who they say they are online? Don't people lie? Let's get this out of the way now, because I know you've heard all the horror stories and some of you are convinced that everyone online is a liar.

The best way to answer that question is by asking another question: Do people lie in the RT world? The answer is a resounding *Yes*. Why would we think that by some strange, mystical machination of the computer, people automatically become saints the moment they connect to an online service? And by that same line of reasoning, why would we think people automatically become devils the moment they sign on?

While no one will dispute that it's much easier to lie in the online world, you'll find that, in general, people who are essentially truthful in the RT world will be truthful in the online one. Conversely, people who lie in the RT world will, likewise, lie in the online one.

41

The Most Common Lies

It's a fact that in the quest for love, we take some lies for granted. We even laugh about them. Women often lie about their age and weight and, as a man, you might tell a woman you make more money than you do or are more successful. We also may be guilty of saying we like something we really don't, or overlooking small faults in a prospective partner just to get the relationship off the ground. I do believe it's called, "Being on your best behavior." You'll find that when it comes to matters of the heart, people online tell the same kind of lies they do in the RT world. But keep in mind that if you're seriously looking for a mate, lying is not the way to go about it. Eventually the truth does come out.

Having said that, let's explore a couple of very good reasons why you may encounter lying online:

Fear

Any woman who has been involved in the online community has heard about the dangers of prematurely giving out personal information. Because it's possible that you're a stalker, a rapist, or a serial killer, she may be understandably leery about saying anything at the beginning to enable you to locate her. Now, it might be easier if she told you her fears up-front, but she doesn't want to appear to accuse you of something and possibly hurt your feelings, so she'll make something up. Once she gets to know you better and tells you the truth and the reasons why she lied to you, you should certainly be understanding about why she did it.

You, of course, shouldn't ask such personal questions so quickly. You should be enjoying your online time with this potential mate; get to know her, be sensitive to her needs and possible fears, and learn to sense when the time is right for requesting the information you'll need to speak to and possibly meet this woman in the RT world.

Public Personalities

There are many public personalities who roam the online community. Now, I'm not necessarily talking about those superstars or big-name politicians we all know, but local personalities—people who are known in their immediate area. These people may include doctors, lawyers, or reporters. If you come from a town with a population of 35, it's safe to say that everyone in that town is a public personality.

A public personality is anyone who is legitimately concerned that knowledge of their online escapades could damage their reputation in the community at large, especially if those escapades include cybersex. Because they may be more easily located than the average online subscriber, they have an obvious interest in keeping personal information a secret.

I once met a very nice lady who initially told me she came from an entirely different part of the country than she did. She not only fabricated her hometown, but also her name and a fairly complete bio. However, as she got to know me, she told me the truth. It turned out she was very well known where she lived. We went on to have a very good online, telephone, and RT relationship.

There are, of course, reasons for lying that have no justification, and people online who lie just for the sake of lying. Learning how to spot these people can save you a lot of headaches, money, and time. They include:

The Online Player

Some people lead a total fantasy life online and will never tell you anything real about themselves, no matter how long you speak to them. They are very good at involving you in their "real" problems, pressing the emotional hot buttons and stringing you along if you let them. They know a man's sexual fantasies and come on to you in a very sexual and alluring way. Before you know it, you're roped into a cybersex relationship in which you are being drained emotionally, and which is going nowhere. You need to be very careful with women who are primarily interested in online sexual play. I've never met one who was the least bit interested in an RT relationship. Fortunately, I have also met very few of this type of person.

Your best defense against this type of player is knowing what you're about and what you're doing online at any given time. Any relationship that has potential should grow and develop at a certain rate. This is just as true in the online world as it is in the RT one. When you are developing an online relationship, you should expect consistency, a sense of responsibility, and, at a certain point, a sharing of RT information, including a phone number. If you don't feel the relationship is progressing in a manner that is comfortable to you, it's really best just to move on. There are too many honest people online who are seriously looking for a mate to waste your time with one of these people.

43

Plain Old Con People

The con person is interested in the quick score. They are not looking for emotional satisfaction—their goal is financial. The con person will try all kinds of tricks to get you to divulge your credit card number, password, or get money out of you. Telling you that he or she is an employee of the online service and that your account is in jeopardy unless you divulge your password is a standard ploy. No employee of any online service will ever ask you what your password is, nor should you ever give your password to anyone. If anyone asks for your password or other financial information, you should report that person to the online authorities immediately.

Married People Posing as Singles

In today's world, it's not just men who make believe they're single; women do it, too. They cruise the online highways and byways just as they do in the RT world, unmindful or uncaring about the emotional pain this type of charade can cause. However, it's even easier for a person to pass as single in the virtual world than in the RT world, because it can be done right from the comfort of home. Any person who passes herself for something she is not is not a suitable partner.

Just as in the RT world, finding out the truth is often difficult, but never impossible. Everybody is subject to external time constraints. Married women are certainly no different. You can often get an idea of a person's external life by the time of day that person is online. If she is online mostly during the day, for example, the chances are higher that she is married. If she avoids meeting you online nights or weekends, the chances are higher that she is married. Does she sign off suddenly in the middle of conversations? You have to wonder who walked into the room who she didn't want knowing she was talking online. Little by little, small facts begin to add up, and the truth of that person's RT world becomes plain.

Children Posing as Adults

It's highly unlikely that in the normal course of conversation online you'll be fooled into believing that a 10-year-old is really 21. However, just like in the RT world, there are 15 and 16-year-olds out there who can act much older than they actually are. Occasionally, you may run into one of them. There is very little danger in ending up in a long-term virtual relationship with a minor. It is only the online "one-night stands"

44

where an inadvertent entanglement can occur. That can be seriously disappointing, not to mention guilt inducing, if you later discover you've been dealing with someone underage.

Keeping your conversation on the adult, non-sexual level at the beginning is a good defense against making this kind of error. A minor cannot sustain for long an in-depth conversation about adult "things." You know, those things we deal with everyday: jobs, salaries, bills, responsibilities, past relationships, marriages, divorces, and children. If you are speaking to someone who claims to be in your generation, you will both share common historical memories you can discuss. If the answers are not what you would expect, then it's best just to say good night and move on.

It's Really Just Common Sense

When you meet a person for the first time in an RT club or bar, you have no idea whether or not that person is telling you the truth. When you deal with a stranger, you use your common sense. That's a given. If something doesn't seem right, you take the appropriate steps to extricate yourself from the situation.

Exercise common sense in the RT world and you have a better chance of staying out of trouble. Exercise it in the online world and you also improve your chances.

It's not as difficult to get an initial sense of that person you're talking to as it may appear. Ask about the weather where that person claims to live. It seems like a very innocuous question, but you can verify the weather. If she says it's 90 degrees with thunderstorms and you check the Weather Channel and find out it was 75 and sunny, something's wrong. If you've been to the part of the country she claims to be from, talk about the landmarks. You'll see if she knows what she's talking about, or if she's trying to steer the conversation in another direction. Just be alert. It's impossible to sustain a lie for any length of time.

initial ⑤
approaches

Words are the most important commodity in the online environment. Whether those words express language, thoughts, or actions, it is through the words you type and the words that a potential mate types back to you that communication, knowledge of each other, and understanding are reached. Ironically, just a few years ago scholars and intellectuals were predicting the demise of the written word in view of the seemingly awesome power of visual media. Now we have come full circle, and the written word, which you compose and send online, has once again taken a powerful position in our daily lives. The pen, or in this case, the keyboard, is mightier than the sword, or in this case, the boob tube.

One might reasonably wonder how moving and complete a conversation carried on entirely with written words can be. In our RT lives, we "hear" a lot more than words. We hear inflections, pauses, and subtle tones of voice that tell us more than the words themselves; we make eye contact or not; we fold our arms or cross our legs in a closed posture; we lean backwards or forwards to show passivity or assertiveness. In short, communication takes place on many different levels, all of which we analyze to determine what the other person is saying to us.

In your RT experience with women, you've learned to rely on these subtle clues for direction. She doesn't have to tell you directly if she wants to spend an evening with you. You can tell by the way she tilts her head when she looks at you, or the way she lightly touches your shoulder. She gives you non-verbal clues that let you know if it's OK to ask her out. Yet, in the online world all of this is missing. How can mere written words convey our true feelings?

Well, if written words were unable to communicate all that exists in the human condition, then books would never be written, and they would certainly never be read. Yet, how often do you pick up a good book and find that you can't put it down? The power of the words forces you to turn page after page.

Until the fairly recent invention of the telephone, many relationships were carried on by the exchange of letters. Today's interactive form of communication is just a modern-day version of yesterday's love letter. We have, as a movie title once suggested, gone back to the future.

In a sense, when you enter the online environment, you have to think of yourself as part character and part author, entering an interactive play in which you play a role written by the other characters *and* help write the script. Shakespeare aptly said that all the world's a stage and all of us merely players. He was definitely talking about the online environment.

The first thing to do is develop an opening that draws the object of your interest into a conversation. Since you're not writing to a mass market, don't use some pat lines that you can use over and over again. You're writing to a market of one: The woman behind that one character you wish to approach. That takes some knowledge of that one-person market.

The More You Know

You'll be so much more successful approaching someone if you already know something about her, especially if you can find some common ground. In the RT world, you often have to fly blind when approaching a woman—stumbling for something witty and intelligent to say, groping for some common interest, experiencing long pauses in the conversation because you don't know what to say next. Fortunately, the online environment gives you many opportunities to find something out about that woman you want to speak to before you speak to her. There are descriptive screen names, profiles to look at, chat rooms where you can observe the way that woman interacts with others, personal home pages to check, photo libraries (if she has one in there), and forums she might post to.

So, throw away those old pat pick-up lines that you use in the RT world. They don't work there anyway, and they certainly won't work in the virtual world. The fact is, there can be so much information available about a person before you speak to her, my belief is most women will almost expect you to know something about them.

48

The first thing to do when you spot someone interesting in a chat room is get some information. At least check her profile, if that service is available. If her profile mentions that she has a home page or indicates she has a photo on file, look at those things first (I know you'll look at the photo without my mentioning it).

If she doesn't have a profile, or that capability isn't available, go into the chat room and observe her. See how she interacts with others in the room; try to get an idea of the personality and character of the woman behind the screen name. Always remember that the real connection is made with the real person behind the screen name. I have gone so far as to enter a chat room under a different name (in those places that allow you to), observe until I'm satisfied, sign off, sign back on under my preferred name, and then initiate a conversation with the woman. Is that stalking? Is that being unscrupulous? No. It's just bettering the odds of success. But I would never start a relationship with a woman under one name, and then try to pick her up using a different name to see if she is who she claims to be. That is unscrupulous.

Once you gather some information, you'll be able to phrase your approach in a way that makes a definite connection. She'll at least know that you've taken a few moments to find out something about her as a person. This is important. When you make that initial contact with a woman and you show an interest in something that she says she likes, you draw her into a conversation with you.

If your initial contact expresses only your needs, you will not be drawing her into a conversation. Never start a conversation with "I want to date you/have cybersex with you/marry you..." or any other "I want" that expresses only your needs and shows no consideration for hers.

This is true for any of the three basic ways you can approach a woman online. The first two are interactive, the third is passive. These are:

- ◉ The Chat Room Approach
- ◉ The Private Message Approach
- ◉ The E-mail Approach

Let's take a look at each approach and see how you can use each one to your advantage.

The Chat Room Approach

Now that you have some idea of what goes on in a chat room, you may wonder how anyone ever meets anyone online. It can certainly be confusing, but chat rooms have a specific and important place in the online environment. They serve as a central meeting point where people of like minds gather to play. Since most chat rooms have a theme, you increase your chances of meeting a woman who shares your interests in a chat room—as long as it's a theme you're interested in.

Of course, just sitting in a chat room does nothing for you if you're not actively involved. The things that you can become involved in are conversation, scene-playing, and role-playing. If you're a regular you'll probably participate in scene- or role-playing more than if you're a visitor, because you'll know all the people. These activities by themselves won't help you meet a woman, but they do give you the ability to bring a woman into the action in a friendly, non-threatening manner. The same can be said about participating in a group conversation. Once you're involved in one, you can talk to a number of women in a friendly manner, or attempt to bring a woman into the conversation.

It's much easier to meet a woman by taking part in the group activity than it is to strike off on your own. I've seen many men enter chat rooms and try to blatantly pick up a woman as though he were having a private conversation with her, without knowing the first thing about the room topic or the woman. That approach is rarely successful, and women who respond are doing it more for sport than for any serious intention. What you want to achieve in a chat room approach is just to make an initial contact and get some sort of favorable response. However, the object of having some general public dialogue with a woman in a chat room is to take the conversation private as quickly as possible.

Going from Public Chat to Private Chat

You have exchanged some simple pleasantries with a woman in a chat room. You have found out something about her, either through her room chat with you and others, from her profile, or from her screen name. You really would like to speak to this woman out of earshot of the other people in the room.

Recall the comparison I made to the RT party. Imagine you have approached a group in which one of the members is a woman you'd like to get to know.

50

You've had a nice conversation with the group as you attempt to make eye contact with the woman. She knows what you're up to, as do the other members of the group. You want to pull her away from the group.

What do you do? Do you wait and hope she turns to you and says, "It's hot in here, would you care to join me on the veranda?" That may happen in the movies—and when it happens in real life, it's wonderful—but the chances for you aren't good. More likely you'll have to say something like, "Would you like to see what's at the buffet table?" Then, what do you do if she says no?

In the online environment, you also want to pull that woman away from the group and have a more private conversation. Fortunately it's much easier online than in the RT world, because you can have a private conversation with her via the private messaging system without physically separating her from the group.

The other important difference is that you can talk to her privately almost immediately after you make initial contact. In fact, I highly recommended it. Once you make one or two exchanges, you can and should take the conversation private. Since you're already in a conversation (a public one), the two easiest and non-intrusive ways of bringing the conversation private are 1) Responding to her next question via the private messaging system or 2) Asking your next question via the private messaging system. Once she responds privately it's unlikely to become public again, and during the private conversation you can find out a lot about her and she about you.

While there is some risk in taking a public conversation private, the consequences of failure are certainly not as devastating as they can be in the RT world. The *worst* she can do is type into the room, "No, GooodeEgg, I don't want to talk to you privately," so everyone can see you've made an attempt and have failed miserably. Your face may get a little red at the computer screen, but it's not the same as being turned down in front of people in the RT world. It's more likely that she'll respond to any intelligent comment you make to her privately.

The Private Message Approach

Whether you start your conversation with her in public or initiate one using the private message system, all of your real online conversations will take place through this system. Basically, a private message is just what it sounds like—a message you can send to another person that can only be read by that other person. Every large online service, many small ones, and the Internet's IRC have this capacity. Of course, the other person has to be signed on to the same service you are in order for you to send a private message.

Unlike taking a public conversation private, initiating a conversation using the private message system is somewhat like making a cold sales call. Your message appears on that woman's monitor screen totally out of the blue. But unlike a sales call, in which your initial response is to hang up as soon as you hear their unending stream of words, a woman will probably read the message before deciding to respond or not. So that first message is critical to your success.

The private message approach has a number of technical advantages over the chat room approach. You're not confined to having conversations with just the people in any particular chat room. You can talk to anyone in the chat area, or in some cases anyone signed on to the service, as long as you know the other person's screen name. The private message is more attention-grabbing than words typed into a chat room, since it pops up on the other person's screen—it's much harder to ignore. On AOL and Prodigy the arrival of a private message is also announced audibly if the other person has a PC speaker or a multimedia setup. So, that provides an additional pull to read the private message.

But just because the online service helps you make your message technically attractive, a woman won't respond to it if you don't make it interesting. Since most real conversations take place via private messages, you can bet that when your message arrives, she'll already be involved in a number of conversations. Audio-visual pyrotechnics aside, your message may just end up in the long queue of other private messages waiting interminably for a response.

To get a response, your approach needs to make an immediate connection—every sales pitch needs to have a hook. Without that, you'll never close a sale. Maybe you don't want to think of yourself as a salesman, but in a very real sense your first private message to a woman is an attempt to sell yourself.

If you think about good selling techniques, they're never centered around the seller. Has a real estate salesperson ever told you to buy a house because he or she is going to make $20,000? Of course not. The focus is always on the buyer. The *hook* is the successful connection between the buyer's needs and the sale object.

52

Your initial private message to a woman also needs these two elements: a focus on her and a connection (albeit a subtle one) between her needs and you. The way to keep the focus on her is to say something complimentary about her. The way to make a connection is to get information about her and find the thing(s) you have in common. Fortunately, the online system allows you to do both quite easily:

◉ As I've already noted, many services allow people to have profiles you can check, so if that's available, you should do that first.

◉ Chat rooms have themes and the people in them share similar interests; even if you're not in the same chat room as the woman you are messaging, you should be familiar with that chat room's topic.

◉ Everybody also has a screen name that says something about the person.

> Making a connection means directing your comment to a point of known common interest. All the direct and indirect information available online should help you find that point of common interest.

Last but not least, there is the hook, the thing that draws a person into the conversation. You can send the wittiest comment across the wires to a woman but if it doesn't leave room for a response, it doesn't have a hook. And basically that's what a hook is—a comment that allows for a response. The hook can often be no more complicated than a statement followed by a question. A question seeks an answer and challenges the recipient to respond; a statement is flat by comparison.

> Compare these two approaches directed to BlkRaven, who has indicated she has an interest in the poetry of Edgar Allen Poe:

```
Good evening, BlkRaven. Love Poe. One of my favorite
authors too. I've read all his poetry.
```

To

```
Good evening, BlkRaven. Has the tempter sent you to rouse
me as I lay napping with your gentle tapping at my chamber
door? Please don't answer Nevermore :)
```

Both show the sender is intelligent, both keep the focus on the woman's interests, and both show the connection between the sender and the woman's interest. But the second one does it in a more indirect way, showing the common interest by using some exact words (in boldface) from Poe's *The Raven*. Plus the playful question invites the woman likewise to respond in a playful fashion.

> The second one also dares to be sensual, without being overtly sexual, while the first one is a closed statement that only offers information. If

the situation allows for it, it's okay to be sensual. After all, we're not trying to cultivate a new business associate, we're trying to start a romance. Below we'll look at some sexual approaches that are never, *never* successful.

Now, I'm not a Poe scholar, and while I've read *The Raven*, I certainly couldn't quote from the poem. How did I get a copy of it to use for my approach? From my extensive book collection? Not at all. I used the considerable resources available to me right online. I went to one of the World Wide Web's search engines (in this case I used AltaVista at http://www.altavista.com), asked it to search for Edgar Allen Poe, and in about two minutes I had a copy of *The Raven*.

It's amazing to me that with all the resources and information available, men still insist on using the same tired pick up lines over and over again. It's not useful. If you use the same line on a woman named GoodGirl4U in the Christian Singles chat room and a woman named FemmFatale in the Bedroom Intimacy chat room, you'll waste a lot of evenings typing into the cybervoid. Always keep these points in mind and you'll cut through the competition and increase your chance of success a hundredfold:

◉ Show intelligence (writing in complete sentences helps).

◉ Use the resources available to get information.

◉ Focus on the woman's interests.

◉ Make the connection.

◉ Don't forget the hook.

It's equally amazing to me how many men insist on using blatantly sexual approaches to women, but I figure they're not really interested in meeting a woman, just insulting her. Perhaps they don't know any better, but you do. Here are some lines that are doomed to failure:

```
Hey, BlkRaven, I want your bod in private.
You turn me on, BlkRaven, let's do cyber.
```

Recently a woman asked me, "What is it about signing on to an online service that turns an intelligent, college-educated man into a hormone-raging adolescent?" I wish I had an answer for her; I'm not a social psychologist but it does seem to be true. If you get nothing else out of this book, get this: Women do not want to speak to men who act like hormone-driven teens.

Another approach seen quite often that's more well-intentioned but equally doomed to failure is this one:

```
Hi. I'm 6' 1", 200#, 26, athletic build, blond hair, blue
eyes, love to surf, live in So. Cal.
```

So, what else is new? This might be acceptable in a newspaper personal ad, but this is live, one-on-one interactive chat. A woman wants to know what's in your *mind*, not what your mind is in. Get a conversation going with a woman first and all the physical description stuff will come later. Once you send a private message to a woman, keep in mind that she's probably already engaged in a number of conversations and it may take her a few minutes to respond. Be patient. You can use the time to send a message to another woman. Nothing says you can't have more than one conversation going at the same time.

In fact, if it does take her a while, it's a good indication that she is involved in other conversations. The speed at which someone responds to you can also be a good indication of how much of her attention you have. If you notice less and less of a delay between your comments and hers, you can feel pretty confident that you made a good connection and you're easing out the competition.

The E-Mail Approach

Not everyone can boldly go where no man has gone before and chat it up in a chat room while everyone is watching, or try to find witty things to say to a woman using the private messaging system. The online environment does not make us into different people, and the fact is, many people are naturally shy.

If you're the shy type or the strong silent type, take heart; you don't have to watch the woman of your dreams slip through your fingers just because you can't get the words together in live chat. There is a way to find a woman in a chat room and get in touch with her without speaking to her "live"—send her an e-mail letter! Of course, you don't have to be shy to use this technique. Sometimes you're just about to shoot off a private message to some interesting lady and she's gone! Signed off. Since there's no way to know when you'll see her again, you can send her an e-mail letter.

55

(Sorry, you can't use this approach on Prodigy because a person's chat name is not associated with that person's e-mail name unless that person allows it. Sadly, if you're in the middle of a conversation and you get *booted*—lose your connection to the service due to a technical difficulty—that person may sign off before you sign back on and you may never find that person again. Oh, well. Still, Prodigy is a wonderful service and a great place to meet a woman.)

There are some basic items to keep in mind when writing an e-mail letter that you hope will catch someone's eye and that will get you a response:

◎ Make the subject line snappy and interesting. (This is especially true if you're writing to a woman you discovered using a dating service.)

◎ Compliment her.

◎ Be real.

◎ Be conversational.

◎ Don't list your qualifications as if you're applying for a job; weave them into the letter.

◎ Minimize physical characteristics; concentrate on more substantial aspects of your personality and character.

◎ Be sure to have your profile on services that have that facility. You can bet your bottom dollar that any woman getting a letter will check your profile before she responds.

With these points in mind, let's look at a couple of scenarios and sample letters.

E-Mail to a Woman You've Observed Online

Here's the scenario:

You're in the chat area hanging out, browsing through who's online when a name, a profile, whatever, catches your eye. Something clicks inside your head and you know you've found someone interesting. You enter the chat room she's in to observe her and, yes, from what you see her saying to others, she certainly does appear to be someone you'd like to get to know a little better.

Perhaps it's the way she says hello to everyone who enters the room; perhaps it's the way other members of the room seem to like her and respect her. Whatever it is, you know you want to speak to her more. Still, you can't bring yourself to do it. After you sign off, take some time to compose a letter to her, telling her a little about yourself and why you think you have something in common with her. The letter in the following example shows what you might say.

```
**E-mail To Woman You've Observed Online**
To:              ZestyyOne
Subject:         Amazed in Sensual Melange
Dear ZestyyOne,

It was really a great pleasure to be in Sensual Melange
earlier this evening because I had the opportunity to
*overhear* your conversation. There were so many times I
wanted to agree with you and just as many times I wanted
to send you a private message but just couldn't bring
myself to do it. I'm ordinarily not tongue-tied around
women but I must admit feeling a bit like a child in awe
around you. Perhaps it is that feeling that compels me to
write this letter. I do know that I would like the oppor-
tunity to get to know you a bit better online and so I'm
writing this letter by way of introduction.

I particularly enjoyed listening to your insightful views
on co-parenting arrangements. As you rightly noted, how-
ever, many divorcing parents seem all too willing to "use
their children as hostages" to get what they want. As a
divorcee and father of two wonderful children, I can speak
from personal experience. Fortunately, cooler heads pre-
vailed and I now share a full and wonderful relationship
with my children. A fact that thrills me. As a psycholo-
gist, I have seen—more than once—the battle scars these
acrimonious divorces leave on these innocent victims.

Well, here I am pontificating—and I don't even know you,
although for some strange reason I feel I do. Please for-
give me, but it's not too often I get the chance to share
my personal views so openly. All I usually get to do is
try to patch up the damage post-trauma. And I have to
remain neutral, at that!
```

I would certainly like the opportunity to speak to you further and explore mutual interests. I do hope you'd like that also.

Sincerely,

Richard

E-Mail to a Woman You Found in a Membership Search

Many services have membership directories that can be prime sources for finding a woman with similar interests. People who put information on the service understand that all other members have access to it, so getting a letter from a stranger is not unusual. In fact, it is fairly common for people to do searches and send e-mail to people who fit their search criteria.

The ease with which it can be done, however, is also its bane. It's okay to make a letter sound like a form letter if you're contacting somebody who has an interest in antique cars, but if your interest is decidedly romantic, anything that looks even slightly like a form letter will *not* be responded to. In fact, the first thought a woman will have upon receiving a letter like this is that it *is* a form letter.

The most important thing for you to accomplish in this letter is to dispel the idea that she has just received a form letter. The way to do that, of course, is to personalize every letter you write and limit your letters to just a few at a time. If you get no response from the first group, then send out a few more, and so on until you work your way through the list. The chances are good, however, you'll get a response long before you finish the list.

Here's the scenario:

You just conducted a search in which you were seeking single women from Des Moines, Iowa, who have an interest in rock and roll. You got a list of 20 possibilities. Scrutinize the possibilities carefully and pick the three you like the best. The following figure gives you an example of a letter you might write to a woman you found in a membership directory search. (Keep in mind that on some online services like AOL, one person can have as many as five screen names, so look at all the profiles carefully. If any of them say almost the same thing, it may be the same person; if you have any doubts, take those off the list. The last thing you want to do is send something you say is not a form letter to the same person twice!)

E-mail To Woman You Found In A Membership Search

To: MusicMaiden

Subject: One In A Million

Dear MusicMaiden,

My heart just sang with joy when I did a membership search for single women in Des Moines who have a love of rock and roll. And, admittedly, while you were not the only woman who was revealed in my search, you were certainly one of the very, very few with whom I saw so many connections. Thus, this letter and the reason for that particular sub-ject line, which is not only the name of a classic love ballad by Johnny Horton (do you know it???) but describes perfectly the way I feel.

I remember listening to that song on the radio as a child and thinking that's the way a man should feel about the woman he loves—like she was one in a million. Perhaps I should have shed those childhood fantasies about life and love long ago but I guess I'm still a bit of a romantic because here I am still single and still looking for that one in a million lady. Can you be the one?

It does appear at first blush that we have a lot of things in common, not the least of which is our mutual love of rock n roll. In fact I love it so much that I've been known to strip off the old business suit, don a pair of cut up jeans and a tie-dye T-shirt and, with electric guitar in hand whip crowds of tens to a frenzy at some of the local Des Moines clubs. That's me: CPA by day, rocker by night. And who says CPAs are a stuffy breed only con-cerned with number crunching? Actually when you think about it, math and music have a lot in common—after all, what is music but math in the form of chords, meter and rhythm?

But, from reading your profile, our mutual interests don't
stop there. We also share an interest in classical litera-
ture, ecology and our birthdays are only days apart. Of
course, we both live in the wonderful city of Des Moines,
and we may have even unknowingly passed each other on the
street or have been just an aisle apart at Tower Records
one Saturday morning.

I don't know if I could be your one in a million man but
I'm hoping this letter will kindle a desire in you to
start the process of finding out and that you'll decide to
write back.

Sincerely,

Richard

Non-Verbal Communication

Not everything you say will be said in words. In the online world, emotions are often expressed by the use of symbols, called *smileys*. Also,
since it takes so much time to type words, abbreviations are used ex-
tensively. Obvious ones, like "u" (for "you") need no explanation, but
you will encounter some that seem mystifying if you're new. The following table shows some common smileys and abbreviations you'll use
in your online life.

Smileys and Abbreviations

:-) or :)	The basic smiley.
;-) or ;)	A wink.
:-(or :(	A frown.
:-/	Skeptical.
:-o	Uh oh!
%-6	Brain-dead.
:-O	Oops.
:*	A kiss.
—"—"—@	A rose.
{{{{{( )}}}}}	A hug or embrace, with the person's screen name placed inside the innermost parentheses.
"g" or "s"	Grin or smile.
btw	By the way.
brb	Be right back.
lol	Laughing out loud.
rofl or roftl	Rolling on the floor laughing.
nac	Naked at computer.

Dating — 6
The online
way

I n the RT world, a date may consist of taking a woman to a restaurant, going to the movies, a show, or a club. Afterwards, you may take her for cappuccino and dessert. Perhaps there will be an amorous encounter to end it. Perhaps not. There may be some talk about a next date. In the RT world, a date consists of doing physical things together. In the virtual world, of course, you can't do those physical things. But, when you look at the essence of a date, you will be able to see that you can have a date in the virtual world just as you can in the RT one. What is the essence of a date?

When you come right down to it, a date is making plans for a specific day and time and carrying out those plans. Really, it is making a commitment and following through on that commitment. Now that is something you can do online as well as off. You can agree to meet a woman at a specific day and time and follow through. So, the essence of a date is exactly the same in either the RT or the virtual world.

Asking for a Date

You've just had a very pleasant two-hour conversation with a woman. You've talked about your mutually shared interests, your plans, your goals, perhaps there has been some romantic or sexual innuendo interspersed in the conversation. You definitely feel there's potential here and you'd certainly like to see her again. Do you ask her for a date?

63

One of the beauties and pluses of dealing with a woman in the virtual world is that there is no pressure to ask a woman for a date the first time you meet her. In the RT world, at the end of a chance meeting you are more or less constrained to ask for the woman's phone number (which both parties understand is so you can call her for a date), or asking directly for a date. If she responds in the negative, that's pretty much the end of it. You may have just wasted a whole evening. Not to mention that asking that question can produce such a fear of rejection it becomes a major event.

These chance first-meeting concerns just do not exist in the virtual world. In the first place, the conversation you had with this woman may have been perfectly lovely. But you also may have had quite a few perfectly lovely conversations, either consecutively or simultaneously, with a number of different women through the course of an evening. (As she may also.) You certainly can't have several private conversations going on at the same time in the RT world; it's a practical impossibility. So, because of this ability to speak to many women, the fear of being rejected by any one of them should be low. Now, that's not to say your ego may not get a little bruised. I've had women stop talking to me in the middle of a conversation and I get upset—for all of five seconds before I start another conversation.

The second reason is related to the first. Since you both can have many simultaneous conversations going on, you don't have to make a do-or-die play for her exclusive attention the very first time you meet her. In the RT world, she's either talking to you or talking to someone else. Those are the choices. In the virtual world, she can be talking to you and to someone else at the same time. While competition for women is a fact of online life, your initial object when meeting a woman is to attract her attention and keep the conversation going. While it certainly is nice if it appears she's speaking to you exclusively, it's not necessary to strive for that on first meeting, and that should take some of the pressure off.

And finally, when it's time to sign off and you think you should ask that woman you just met for a date—you don't have to. All you really need do is mention that you had a nice conversation with her and ask when she'll be online next. If she's also had a pleasant conversation with you, she has nothing to lose by telling you. After all, it's not the same thing as giving out her phone number. So, the pressure of asking for a date immediately after meeting a woman isn't necessary. Through numerous unofficial meetings and the

64

exchange of e-mail, you will both have the opportunity to get to know each other without pressure.

As your relationship develops, there will come a time when you will want to make more definite plans to meet online. This can certainly be termed a virtual date. By the time this happens, you have both expressed mutual enjoyment in being together, so making a virtual date usually lacks the fear of rejection associated with its RT counterpart.

As I've already noted, a virtual date, in its essence, is the same as dating a woman in RT. There is the act of agreeing upon a day and time; making a plan, such as being in a chat room together and presenting yourselves as a couple, or meeting in a private room for a one-on-one encounter; and following through on what you agreed on. These are the commitments normally associated with virtual dating that are similar to RT. There is one other aspect in a virtual date that has no RT counterpart: Making a virtual date also means that you do *not* employ the private messaging system to engage in conversations with other women.

Can Feelings Really Develop Between People Online?

If you haven't experienced a virtual relationship or had the pleasure of getting to know someone online, it might be difficult to imagine that real feelings can develop between people in this type of environment. But, surprisingly enough, feelings can and do develop. Often these feelings are deep and just as often can happen very quickly.

In the RT world, we often judge people by the way they look. This is certainly true in our search for a mate. Perhaps you've chosen not to speak to a single woman because you didn't think she was pretty enough, or, what's often the case, because she was too pretty and you knew you'd be rejected. Who knows how many chances you've lost at finding love and happiness because of some imagined physical barrier?

The online world, of course, eliminates the barrier often created by physical appearance, simply because we don't see the other person. While we may generally describe our appearance and at some point exchange photos, virtual relationships are based on qualities other than appearance: two people's ability to communicate on the same intellectual and emotional plane, mutual and shared interests, trust, willingness to listen to the other person's needs, appreciation and respect for the other person, and the ability to keep the flame of romance alive.

In short, virtual relationships are often based on the qualities most often associated with successful long-term relationships. And because of the anonymity of an online relationship, people often speak quite freely about their hopes and dreams. So, it should come as no surprise that feelings do develop in virtual relationships.

Of course, every virtual relationship that becomes a potential RT relationship will have to successfully translate itself into the RT world. When you first meet your online love f2f, physical attraction and chemistry come into play. But, once again, it should be no surprise that people who have been honest with each other during their virtual relationship meet each other for the first time with the absolute certainty that they will be physically attracted to each other. Those people have discovered that sexual attraction, just like any other emotion is based, ultimately, not on physical appearance but on the level of the emotional connections they have reached.

I have heard again and again from people who have met each other f2f for the first time after a deep virtual relationship that they were not concerned about being physically attracted to the other. In various but similar words, they have all said, "Oh, no, that was never a concern. The relationship was already there; we had no doubts that we would be physically attracted to each other."

None of this, of course, means that you will live happily ever after. If everyone who fell in love stayed in love, there would never be a divorce. And even people who love each other sometimes find they can't deal with each other day-to-day. It is just important to keep in mind that you can develop real feelings for a woman you've met online, and you can successfully transplant those feelings into the RT world.

Making an Online Relationship Work

Keeping a relationship fresh and exciting in the RT world is more often a product of the energy both partners put into it than the actual love they feel for each other. Love, like a flower, withers when untended. It takes work to keep an RT relationship going. The same can be said about a virtual relationship.

People who have successful online relationships—relationships that progress through the telephone and meeting stages—tend to be people who spend an extraordinary amount of time communicating on many different levels. Of course, there is the direct one-to-one communication you will have online but, for the most part, online time spent together will be the least of the communication you will have. In fact, if that is the only communication you have with a woman, you have little chance of succeeding beyond the virtual stage.

Relationships that have potential use the online service's communication ability to the maximum—and then some. It is not unusual, for example, for online couples to exchange hundreds of e-mail letters before they speak to each other. When you think about the time and effort it takes to write a letter, and what that says about your commitment and desire, you begin to understand the importance of e-mail in an online relationship. Further, think about the impact of a letter—even a brief one saying, "Thinking of you" written before you dash off to work in the morning or before going to sleep at night.

You should not think of or use e-mail only as a means of exchanging information, thoughts, and ideas. Rather, you should think of and use e-mail as the virtual substitute for RT activity. In the absence of being able actually to do something RT, send it off in a letter: "I would really like to hold you right now, but, I can't, so I'm sending you a hug."

Online couples also often show their commitment to each other by using complementary screen names and, where available, by referring to each other in their respective online profiles. In fact, this is a fairly common practice. While complementary screen names often follow the standard RT marriage convention, with the woman incorporating or reflecting the man's name, the only requirement is that the reference appear obvious. The list of screen names in Chapter 4 contained the names LadyOloff and LadysGuy. Anyone seeing those names together in a chat room would automatically know they were a couple. Profiles, of course, offer a more extensive way to refer to your online love. Not only can you refer to her by screen name, you can put in some words of affection for her.

Words, however important, are not the only tools you'll use to make your online relationship successful. You might think that words are all you have, but that's not true. You can also perform deeds in your RT life to indicate to your online partner that you're putting in the effort to make your online relationship work. Renting that video she mentioned the other night and watching it shows her that you're willing to become involved in things she likes. It takes time and effort in your RT life to go to the video store, rent a video, and watch it, but it's effort you would

67

ordinarily put into an RT relationship, isn't it? RT deeds also often make an otherwise virtual relationship more concrete.

The total effect of the words you say to each other and the deeds you perform for each other are a good indication of the level of effort you are both willing to put into your online relationship. You can be sure the effort put into an online relationship can translate to an RT relationship, and it is often effort that gets a relationship through the tough times.

Maintaining More than One Relationship

You won't always want to maintain only one online relationship, or, for that matter, have only online relationships. You may have more than one online relationship, or some combination of online and RT relationships. There's really no reason why you can't date more than one woman at the same time. You haven't made a commitment to any one woman, and at this stage of the process there really is no reason why you should. After all, you haven't met any of them yet—perhaps you haven't even spoken to any of them. You have developed feelings for one or more of them and those feelings are being returned.

The only issues involved here are not how many women you choose to date concurrently but how you present yourself and how the woman reacts.

Honesty is always the best policy when dealing with anyone. The online environment is certainly no different. While there may be some reticence at the beginning about giving out personal information, there is nothing personal about telling someone you are not ready to commit to anyone and that you are seeing, or want to see, other women, whether that be virtual or RT. Building a relationship on a lie is certainly not healthy and indicates that you should in no way be considered a serious mate by the woman or women you are lying to, whether those are online or RT women. Moreover, when dealing with women online, you should never forget there's a living, breathing human being behind the screen name whose feelings can be hurt.

While you can control the way you present yourself, you, of course, can't control the reaction of others. Even if you're honest from the beginning, as a relationship deepens, feelings of jealousy may surface. You might be surprised to learn that jealousy can be an issue in cyberspace, but it very much is. The situation can get more complicated when cybersex is involved. Cybersex, like RT sex, tends to change a person's perspective on the issues and may be perceived by the other party as a commitment, even if you don't. It is probably best to stay completely away from cybersex when you are having more than one online relationship.

When dealing with jealousy, consistency is the best approach. Always follow through with your plans and maintain the level of attention she is used to receiving. Even online, people can feel when they are not being treated fairly and that only exacerbates the situation. If, in fact, your feelings have waned, then you must deal with that honestly and forthrightly. Remember that jealousy is not confined strictly to the other person. You, too, might feel jealous if the situation were reversed.

Determining Serious Prospects

Other than this amorphous feeling of "love," what should you look for in your virtual relationship that will help you determine if it has potential? While everything that you do in the virtual world is written, you can find out a lot about the other person. Here are some things you should look for and/or ask about to help make your decision:

Honesty   One of the most crucial aspects of any relationship, and also one of the most difficult things to determine about the other person in a virtual relationship. Nonetheless, you can get a good sense of whether she is honest by regular and constant communication. Is she consistent? Does she tell you one thing one day and another the next? Does everything she says about her RT life seem logical, or are there big holes in her story? Is her physical description too good to be true? If she has other online friends and you speak to them, do they all have a good opinion of her? When you add it all up, is she credible?

Appreciation   Does she show a willingness to be interested in the things you are? Are her e-mail communications to you full, or just one-liners? Do you have to wait a long time for an e-mail response, or does she seem to respond as soon as she gets your letter? What about your online time together? Do you spend a good deal of time together? When speaking through the private messaging system, does she always take a long time to respond as though she is having other conversations, or does she respond quickly?

Responsibility and dependability   You can certainly get a real sense of whether she is responsible by the way she relates to you. Does she keep her online dates with you and e-mail you when she says she will? Has she ever consented to do something that is essentially outside the domain of your virtual relationship and not follow through? For example, did you both agree to read a book and she never did? You can do many such things together that will prove she is someone you can depend on. In addition, what does she say about her RT responsibilities? Did she ever say she skipped work because she didn't feel like going, or that her house looks like a bomb hit it? Any sense you can get of the way she handles her RT responsibilities is important in determining the potential of a virtual relationship.

Significant others   Does she have RT friends? Are they long-term friendships? Or, are all her friendships virtual? If all her friendships are virtual, you may be dealing with someone who is incredibly isolated or shy, who may never be able to make the transition from a virtual to an RT relationship. What about ex-lovers or ex-spouses? Were they long-term relationships? Why did they end? Is she still on good terms with any of them? How does she appear to relate to her parents and siblings? Does she talk about them lovingly or not?

Financial stability   Does she always complain about spending more on her online bill than she wants to? What can you gather about her RT spending patterns? Do they seem to be in line with her stated income level, or do they appear to be excessive?

Willingness to proceed   Finally, every potential relationship goes through the stages of virtual, telephone contact, and the f2f meeting. While there is no set time period for this progression, most people proceed to the telephone stage within two months of the onset of the virtual relationship. Does she show a willingness to proceed to the next step within a reasonable period of time? If not, what are her reasons? This topic is fully covered in Chapter 8.

Breaking Up Is Hard to Do

There will come a time in your online life when you may have to break up a virtual relationship. Like everything, there is a wrong and a right way of doing things. The wrong way is taking the easy way out—what I call the coward's way—which is very easy to do online. The coward just stops responding to the other person's e-mail letters, and ignores the other person's private messages when both are online together. In extreme cases, the coward will even change his screen name and totally "disappear" into the anonymity of cyberspace. Although you haven't met this other person, keep in mind that you are dealing with a person who has feelings. Just think of how you would feel if this happened to you.

70

The only moral and ethical way to break up with someone online is to deal with her directly and honestly. Perhaps the issue is jealousy because you or she is having more than one virtual relationship. Perhaps you have determined that, based on her responses, the relationship has no potential. Perhaps you have met someone else, either virtual or RT, that you want to pursue exclusively. Whatever your reasons, discuss them with her and hear what she has to say. No relationship is without its problems, and sometimes dealing with problems makes a relationship stronger. You may be able to work things out; you may not. Whatever the outcome, it is always better to break up a relationship maturely.

The chances are good that she will also be mature about it, but emotional situations do not always lend themselves to maturity. You may, for a while, have to deal with quite a few emotional e-mail letters, not all of them complimentary. Respond to these letters calmly but assertively, making sure that you do not give her any double messages about the possibility of resuming your relationship. If you are consistent, she will accept your decision and, if the both of you wish, you could maintain a lasting virtual friendship.

safe ⑦

sex ???

No other aspect of online meeting and mating engenders more discussion and controversy than the act of cybersex. Just about everyone in the online community has an opinion about it. Some people are vehemently opposed to it; others just as vehement in support of it. There's no question that it has RT consequences. Cybersex has broken up RT relationships and marriages, sometimes even being cited in divorce papers. Even though lawyers will tell you that cybersex is legally not adultery, it sure feels that way to a spouse who's been the victim of it. This book offers no opinion concerning the legal and moral issues of cybersex. If you're looking for a mate and, therefore, presumably single, adultery should not be an issue for you.

When you meet a woman online, you may at some point engage in cybersex. Not every woman you'll meet online will "do cyber" as they call it, and perhaps you won't either. But it may also be worth the experience, even just once. I would caution you, though, that cybersex is not risk-free. Despite the air of anonymity, casualness, and unreality it has about it, cybersex can, and often does, trigger real emotions and, as such, has the ability to trap you in an unwanted relationship. Fantasy is often stronger than reality, and cybersex ranks at the top of the scale as far as fantasies go.

It is not especially wise, therefore, to engage in cybersex with a woman you just met online, and I would be leery about the intentions of a woman who appears to be only interested in cybersex. However, as a natural outgrowth of an ongoing and deeply emotional relationship, cybersex may provide a satisfying outlet to your emotions and allow you to share sensual secrets not normally discussed in everyday conversation.

Hot Chat in a Private Room

You make a date with your lady love to meet in a private room at a certain time. This meeting is going to be romantic, sensual, and sexual—there's no doubt about that. You've developed a longing for each other that has gone way beyond the friendship stage. You may feel a little strange signing on, knowing that you are about to engage in cybersex. How do you begin? How can you transmit sensuality and sexuality via a keyboard and words scrolling up a computer monitor?

Let's look in on a sensual conversation between MachoMan and MachosGal, two people who have dated online for a month but haven't yet proceeded beyond the online state. *Note: Sentences bracketed with* :: *are used to enclose actions or thoughts online, as opposed to dialogue.*

MachoMan:	::It's 8 o'clock. I ring your doorbell.::
MachosGal:	::Walking slowly to door, enjoying that you may be anticipating seeing me. Dressed in knee-length, black silk dress; low cut, showing plenty of cleavage. Single strand of pearls around neck. Red lipstick; blue eye-shadow; little makeup; my long dark hair twisted in a French braid; three-inch black high heels; black sheer nylons; fingernails a dark red. Simple but elegant. Getting to door, opening it slowly. Seeing you. Sensual smile::
MachoMan:	::Returning smile:: Good evening, Melissa. You look ravishing. ::Holding hands behind back. Leaning forward. Warm soft sensual kiss on lips::
MachosGal:	Hmmmmmmmm. ::Softly purring. Wondering what you're hiding behind back:: What are

you hiding, John? Some present for me?
::Holding door open::

MachoMan: ::Stepping inside, closing door:: Could
              be. ::Looking sensually at you, admiring
              your features::

MachosGal: Let me see!! ::Peering behind your back::
              Flowers!!

MachoMan: Roses. Red ones. ::Offering roses to
              you::

MachosGal: My favorite. How sweet. ::Taking roses,
              turning:: I'll get a vase. ::Disappearing
              into kitchen; returning with roses in cut
              crystal vase; placing them on coffee
              table; sitting on couch; patting couch::
              Sit down.

MachoMan: ::Approaching. Sitting close, smelling
              the sweet essence of your perfume::

MachosGal: ::Passion::

MachoMan: ::Gazing deeply into your eyes; stroking
              your cheek with back of hand; feeling
              your soft; smooth skin; running a finger
              down your cheek to your lips; tracing
              your lips with finger::

MachosGal: ::Kissing finger softly as I tingle to
              your touch; nipples getting hard::

MachoMan: ::Feeling you quiver to my touch; finger
              traveling down the long nape of your
              neck, following its curves::

MachosGal: Hmmmm. Your touch turns me on.

MachoMan: Your beauty excites me. ::Stroking bare
              shoulder; upper arm; pulling you close to
              me; kissing you hard on lips; tongue
              crashing through your teeth to meet your
              tongue::

SAFE SEX???

MachosGal::	::Feeling your tongue in my mouth; our tongues touching; intertwining; unbuckling your belt; unzipping pants; feeling your hardness throbbing beneath::
MachoMan:	::Excited; reaching around your back; unzipping dress; tongues dancing with each other; unclasping bra; pulling at dress and bra exposing breasts::
MachosGal:	::Soft moan as dress is undone; pulling at pants to expose your manhood::
MachoMan:	::Getting on knees on couch facing you; allowing pants to fall; kissing your neck softly, caressingly; kissing your shoulder; taking your perfectly formed right breast in hand; squeezing it; stroking it; rolling your hard nipple between my thumb and forefinger::
MachosGal:	::Stroking you; feeling you hard in my hand; so big; desiring to feel you inside me::
MachoMan:	::Taking your breast into my mouth; as much of it as I can; sucking it in; caressing your nipple with my tongue; squeezing your other breast with my hand; stroking it; feeling its hard nipple get harder at my touch::
MachosGal:	::Kissing the top of your head; your hair:: I love the smell of your manliness. ::Pulling you towards me; falling backwards onto couch; holding you; we fall together; you on top of me; panting for you; pulling you towards my lips by your hair; kissing you passionately::
MachoMan:	::Kissing you; your mouth; your checks; your eyes; your nose; engulfing you with kisses; kicking off shoes; pulling off pants; underwear; standing; looking passionately down at you; seeing the desire

```
in your eyes; the sweet hardness of your
breasts; gently taking off your shoes;
pulling your dress completely off; allow-
ing your undone bra to drop to the floor;
pulling your panties off; gazing down
lustfully at your beautiful naked body::
You are perfect. I want you.

MachosGal:        I want you, too.
```

An online session like this one can literally go on for hours, with the intention of coming to a simultaneous climax. Do people really reach a sexual orgasm doing cybersex, or is most of it faked? Years ago, in a scene from the movie *When Harry Met Sally*, Harry and Sally are eating in a delicatessen in New York City, discussing women faking orgasms—not during cybersex but during physical sex. Harry (Billy Crystal), who prided himself on his manly ability to please a woman, boasted that every woman he had ever been with had achieved orgasm during sex. Sally (Meg Ryan) said that most of them were probably faking it. Harry said a woman couldn't fake an orgasm. In this remarkable scene, Sally demonstrated to Harry just how a woman could fake an orgasm, much to the amazement of the other restaurant patrons and to the detriment of Harry's now bruised male ego.

The fact is that most of these "sexual" encounters are probably faked. It wouldn't surprise me in the least if one or both partners were watching television or listening to music during their so-called "passionate experience." Of course, when two intelligent people start misspelling the simplest words in the heat of online passion, a case can be made that something real has, indeed, taken place in this virtual world. That something real may not be the act of sex itself but the sharing of sensual secrets and the consequent closeness that this sharing brings.

Is Cybersex for You?

A lot of people won't do cyber for various reasons; but a lot will. You have to decide for yourself whether you want to engage in cybersex

77

and, if you do, with whom, after weighing the pros and cons. There's no question that, in this age of deadly sexually transmitted diseases, cybersex is as safe as you can get. Physically, that is. However, if you do decide to try it, or engage in it on a regular basis, you should keep in mind that cybersex can be deceptively innocent, and there are costs involved.

Engaging in cybersex is a fantasy and, as Hollywood discovered decades ago, fantasy can be as strong as, if not stronger than, reality. Unless you actually know what the person on the other end really looks like, the chances are you're going to imagine she is beautiful and alluring. Connect that fantasy to that screen name long enough and often enough, and the image you develop takes on a life of its own. If you should one day meet her and the fantasy doesn't match the reality, you can be in for a grave disappointment—and your reaction may disappoint or hurt *her*. On the other hand, developing an intimate virtual relationship with someone you feel compatible with may bring you together emotionally and break down physical barriers.

Cybersex and the Single Woman

If you're looking for a mate in the physical world, when do you expect to begin a sexual liaison with that woman? The first date? After a month? When you get married? The chances are you expect some sexual intimacy at some point after you get to know each other, and have some reasonable expectation that the relationship will continue to develop and grow over time, leading to a commitment.

Relationships online can happen very quickly—a lot quicker than most outsiders to the medium realize. People tend to be very up-front about what they want. They put it in their profiles; they enter chat rooms with suggestive names. The fact is, you can end up in an intimate situation within minutes of meeting a woman. To an online novice, this might be enticing and exciting. To someone just looking for a virtual relationship this might be acceptable.

If you're really looking for a relationship, these quick, intimate adventures are a fantasy trap you should avoid. Once again, you should not underestimate the emotional power of these sexual adventures. Nor should you ignore your real-time sexual experience in understanding that physical attraction often creates relationships that should never have started, and keeps relationships together long after they should end—to the emotional detriment of both partners.

There is another consideration for you who want to find a mate: Would you want to spend the rest of your life with someone who was willing to be intimate with you before she got to know you? The chances are good your answer is, "No."

Cybersex and the Married Woman

Sooner or later you'll run across a married woman who is more than willing to have cybersex, often at a moment's notice. There's really no advantage to you, if you're looking for a mate, to engage in cybersex or any intimate online relationship with a married woman. Married people—men and women alike—who engage in online sex or have intimate online relationships cannot be happy in their own relationships. Personally, I've never believed those personal ads that say, "Have a happy marriage but looking for afternoon delight." No—people who are married and seeking affairs are either bored or miserable, in the RT world as well as the online world.

Engaging in cybersex when you're married may not yet be legally termed adultery, but there is something immoral and unethical about it. When a married woman tells me she's spent the whole day thinking about me, I have to conclude that either she's lying, or I'm playing a part in breaking up a marriage—neither of which is very tasteful to me. The fact is, legal adultery or not, marriages have broken apart because of online affairs, and the whole business can get very messy. If a married woman approaches me proposing an online relationship, my response is "You seem very nice and we can be friends, but if you're unhappy with your spouse, get a divorce and write me in a couple of years when you're ready to have another relationship." Best to stay clear of these entanglements.

Of course, not all married women will *tell* you they're married. Not all married women and men who are looking for affairs mention that they're married in the RT world, so why should you expect people to be more honest in the online world? You shouldn't. And since it's so much easier to pose as something you're not in the online world, it is extremely difficult to determine if that woman on the other end is, in fact, married. Still there are ways to tell.

The best way to protect yourself against ending up with a married woman is to have your own goals clearly in mind. As they say, the best defense is a good offense. When you know what you're looking for you can avoid this trap, or at least minimize it. If you're looking for someone you can be with in the physical world, you're presumably looking for someone who will spend time with you in the online world, both live-time and through the exchange of e-mail. You should certainly not waste your time on someone who is not willing to give you an equal amount of time. Married women, and women who are in live-in situations, will have time constraints placed upon them by their relationships. These time constraints become pretty obvious after a short period of time. Here are some of the clues:

- Does she seem to spend much more time online during normal business hours than she does on evenings and weekends?
- Do her explanations for the time spent away from the computer seem logical and reasonable?
- Does the story of her life, in general, seem logical and reasonable?
- Are her e-mail letters brief or do they appear rushed?
- And last, but certainly not least, when it comes time to exchange phone numbers, does she refuse to give you a phone number, or give you only a work number?

Should you meet a woman online who acts this way, you could be dealing with a married woman. But even if you're not, any woman who cannot be accommodating is not a potential mate.

Can Cybersex Lead to a Good Relationship?

No relationship, either in the RT or the online world, based solely on sex can lead to a good relationship. While sex plays an important part in any relationship, all relationships need to share common interests and have common goals to survive long-term. Having an online relationship provides many opportunities to communicate your thoughts and feelings to another person, by spending online time together privately or in chat rooms with others who share your interests, and through the exchange of e-mail. You shouldn't waste this valuable opportunity by only engaging in cybersex.

Explore common interests with your potential mate openly and directly and keep cybersex in its place. If you're serious about finding a potential mate, develop those qualities that are important to a relationship: honesty, trust, responsibility, and dependability.

Sensuality vs. Sexuality

There's a big difference between being sensual and being blatantly sexual. Sensuality implies romance, complimenting your partner, being supportive, listening to the needs of your online love. Being blatantly sexual is more about satisfying your own needs. This is especially true in the area of cybersex, where the act of physically touching your online partner is totally absent and, therefore, the ability to physically satisfy that partner does not exist. Engaging in cybersex for its own sake becomes nothing more than an act of self-gratification when sensuality is missing.

As you develop the elements your relationship will need to have a chance of surviving in the RT world, definitely include sensuality in your communication. Show her that you are a romantic, capable of tender love and understanding. When and if cybersex comes—or better yet, its RT equivalent—it will have a fullness to it that mere sex alone can never hope to duplicate.

8 Moving forward

What is the speed at which a relationship can move online? There really is no definitive answer, although it's at least a couple months, on average, before most online couples feel comfortable about talking to each other on the phone and have a desire to do so.

Before you reach that point, you will have created a fairly full and meaningful relationship with that woman on the other end of the computer. You have established mutual trust and respect, and your communication is frequent and interactive. You have enjoyed each other on many levels; perhaps there have been many amorous conversations and letters; perhaps even some cybersex. You could say you've reached a fairly advanced stage in your relationship. You've bonded with that other person. Keep in mind that bonding is very important in a physical relationship, but keep in mind that your relationship is still virtual, although your feelings may be telling you otherwise at this point, and so might hers.

There is absolutely no physical world equivalent to this step of exchanging phone numbers. After all in the physical world, this usually occurs on the first evening of meeting a woman. If you meet a woman in a club and you spend an enjoyable evening with her, if she doesn't give you her phone number or doesn't call you after a week or so, you can just forget it. You might be upset, your ego might be bruised, your wallet might be a little thinner, but there has been no great emotional investment.

83

In the online world, however, there frequently has been a major emotional investment and moving a relationship from the online world to the phone world is a big step in moving your relationship from a potential relationship to an RT one. But it is also a necessary step.

Going to Voice

You and your potential mate should consider a number of factors when deciding if it's time to go to "voice," that is, speak on the phone. The first, of course, is the level of trust that has developed between you. The second is the level of comfort in your interactions and the ease with which those interactions take place. If it's easy to talk to that person online, the chances are good it will be equally easy to do so on the phone. The third is the level of communication. Are there details you'd like to share about your life that are just being missed in your online communications?

The fourth is a desire to hear each other's voice. While it is only natural to, at some point, have a desire to get to know each other's voices, I put this fourth because this desire is really the product of the other three. If the other three reasons are not in place first, then the desire to hear each other's voice, by itself, should not be the most compelling reason to go to voice.

You might say that the inflection in a person's voice is an important part of judging that person, and I agree. But we are also talking about a person with whom you have already developed a relationship. Inflection will add another dimension to that relationship and help you confirm what you already know, but it won't start a relationship that isn't there or end one that is. Besides, how often have we heard a woman's voice on the phone and tried to figure out what she looked like based on her voice only to be completely wrong?

Let's go back to that third reason. Even though I tucked it in the middle of the others, it's actually one of the most important reasons to go to voice. Online communication, both live chat and e-mail, provides an excellent way to get to know the core of another person. You can discuss your goals, your dreams, your desires, your likes, your dislikes—all the essential things. You'll also be able to talk about your life in general—but that's also where online communication fails: in its ability to communicate the many, often mundane, details that occur in our daily lives.

You'll certainly be able to tell your online love that you went to work, had some words with the boss, had a meeting at 2:00, and then went to the supermarket before you came home—but will you really be able to tell her in detail *everything* that happened? Unless you're a prolific writer or have tons of free time, you probably won't. These details add color to your dealings with others, and the *details* are frequently missing in your online communication. These may not seem so important at the beginning of your relationship, but as the relationship becomes more involved, they get increasingly important. When you find yourself wishing you had more time to tell her all these details and feel empty that you don't, you have reached the stage in your relationship to speak on the phone.

Hopefully, she'll feel the same way at the same time. One way to find out is to mention that you'd like to tell her about all the small, detailed things that go on in your life but find the present form of communication inadequate, and were wondering if she had the same desire. And, hey, it's OK to tell her you'd like to hear the sound of her voice. This is a romance, after all. It may be that she'll bring up the subject first, in which case, you're all set. Just get the number, sign off, and dial.

Overcoming Telephone Obstacles

Because this is often the first step in actualizing a potential relationship, there are sometimes obstacles to overcome. It's important to recognize the motivation behind some of these obstacles so you can deal with them effectively and without disruption. Let's take a look at what you may have to face:

She's Not Ready

If both parties in a relationship were always ready to do the exact same thing at the exact same time, we would be living in an ideal world. Unfortunately, that's not the case. She may not feel the relationship has advanced to the point that she feels comfortable talking over the phone. Although this may come as a surprise, the best approach to helping her be ready is to accept her decision and act rationally and reasonably.

Discuss the situation openly, and listen to her reasons for not wanting to make voice contact at the present time. You may not agree with her, but she's not asking for your opinion. Don't

try to offer her any fixes; nothing's broken. We men often try to fix things when all a woman wants us to do is listen. This is one of those times. Just listen and back off for awhile. Don't worry—she won't forget you want to speak to her, and she'll be thinking about it. You might be surprised when, after a couple of weeks, she tells you that she would like to speak to you over the phone.

She's Uneasy about Giving You Her Phone Number

There are a number of reasons she may be uneasy about taking this step (we'll assume she's not married and afraid her husband will answer the phone), some of which may have nothing to do with you:

Lack of trust   Trust is the key element in any relationship, online or off. Have you proven yourself to be trustworthy? Have you followed through on all your online commitments with her? Have you kept your appointments and promises? If not, then she probably won't exchange phone numbers with you. Would you in her position? If you have, then keep reading.

Loss of control   Even though you have both shared personal details of your lives, when it comes time to give you that one bit of crucial information that will allow you to enter her home in a way she won't so easily be able to control, she may balk. After all, once you have her phone number, you'll be able to use it anytime.

Other people's horror stories   She may have heard bad stories from other women online who gave out their phone numbers and regretted it. When the source of her unease cannot be directly traced back to some action on your part, then the answer to any of the above is to give her your phone number and invite her to call you, collect if necessary. If you also have a problem with giving her your phone number, then you should not have brought the subject up in the first place. Reassess this relationship in light of this development and decide whether you want to continue to pursue it.

If she doesn't call at the agreed upon time, you should also reassess the relationship. Keep in mind that mutual responsibility is an important part of any relationship and if she can't follow through on this act, a red flag should go up. If you've really come to like this woman, you may want to ask her why she didn't call but, regardless of her answer, the fact remains that she didn't follow through on an important commitment, and I would certainly have my doubts about ever actualizing this relationship in RT. What you shouldn't do is allow your imagination to run away with you over giving out your phone number to someone who now doesn't appear to be the person you thought she was. And if you followed my advice about having that second phone line installed, you really should not be concerned at all.

She's Afraid of the Reality

I'm sure we've all run into situations in our physical lives where we've tried to turn a friendship with a woman into something romantic only to be told that she likes the friendship so much she would be afraid to lose it if it didn't work out romantically. That's probably just a polite way of saying she doesn't see us in that light, but sometimes it's true. Friends are important. This situation is similar, except that your relationship is already romantic.

What it boils down to is fear of transition, moving from one level to the next. Needless to say, this is not a fear exclusively felt by women. You may also have this fear, but since we're talking about you asking to speak to the woman on the telephone, I'm going to assume that this is not your problem.

The fact is, she may be so comfortable with the online relationship that she is afraid that if it doesn't go well over the phone, she'll lose something that's become important to her. This is a big fear that needs to be overcome if the relationship can ever progress. And this is also why there has to be a certain time limit within which an online relationship should take this step— too long and you run into this difficulty.

When confronted with this obstacle, remind your online love—gently of course—that you feel the relationship has progressed to the point where it needs to move to this level. Tell her that life is about taking risks, and that proceeding to the telephone is a risk worth taking and a step designed to further enhance and enrich the relationship. Mention all the positive aspects of making this move.

Don't say anything like, "Even if it doesn't work, we can still be online friends." It may seem considerate, but it just smacks of negative reinforcement. Your aim should be to sound positive and upbeat about moving to this next step. Of course, if she asks, confirm that you will certainly be friends with her, but reemphasize that there's no reason why you can't talk as freely over the phone as you have online. Give her your phone number, without asking for hers in return. And give her some time to think about it.

How much time you give her depends on the depth of your online communication with her and how long you have been speaking to her, but in no case should you wait as much time as you've already invested in the relationship. If the time spent has been relatively short—say, two months or less—an additional month should be plenty of time to wait. If, however, you've had a long relationship—say, six months—then a week or two is probably be the most you should wait. I don't actually recommend having an online relationship that long *without* mentioning the subject of voicing. A person who is content with only an online relationship for that long is not going to give you the RT relationship you want.

If, after that period of time, she still doesn't want to speak to you over the phone, you should just politely tell her that you want to find someone to be with in the physical world and will unfortunately have to continue your search. Tell her that you hope she changes her mind and that you'll still consider her a friend, but you really want to find someone you can be with.

She'll Never Give You Her Phone Number

We already discussed the "online player" and other women who, because of other considerations, will never give you their phone number. Hopefully, you'll weeded them out before you get to this stage. But one reason to keep a definite time-frame in mind and constantly assess the level of the relationship is to avoid dealing with one of these types for longer than necessary. We also looked at the pros and cons of conducting an exclusive online relationship versus an open one. Certainly when it gets to this stage, an open relationship provides a hedge against the possibility of not getting a phone contact. On the other hand, you also lose some of the depth of an exclusive relationship.

What I'm talking about in this section is the honest person who wants to have a relationship—until it actually becomes possible. Then they get cold feet. You meet this kind of person in the physical world—quite frequently, actually—and you'll certainly run across them online. They can fit into any of the three fear categories just discussed, or they can have any other valid reason for demurring when faced with speaking to you on the phone. This might sound hard and uncaring, but the bottom line is, the reason doesn't make a difference. She's just not going to give you her phone number—ever. The only thing to be concerned with is when to call it quits.

That point is certainly reached when you've been discussing the exchange of phone numbers for as long as you've been talking online, but should never go on for more than two months. Sadly, you'll just have to break up with this woman and move on, because she just won't ever speak to you on the phone.

Pressure Tactics

Pressure tactics don't work in the physical world. Well, that's not really true—they work, but usually in the opposite direction we intended them to. If they don't work in the physical world, they work even less in the online world.

Remember that no matter how many declarations of love you may have made to each other, it's still *an online relationship with potential*, and nothing more. The glue that holds an RT relationship together—shared memories and experiences—doesn't yet exist. The glue of an online relationship is made up of hopes, expectations, plans. In other words, the future. And the future, by its very definition, does not yet exist. While all of these things can be very strong, when forced up against pressure to do something in the here and now, they can crumble very quickly.

It won't do you any good, therefore, to try to pressure a woman to call you when she's not ready by saying things like, "If you don't give me your phone number now, I'm never going to speak to you again." That just won't work. Don't even bother trying it.

However, keep in mind that there is a difference between a pressure tactic and a statement of fact. And that is your own motivation. When you say something with the express purpose of trying to force someone into an action that person would not otherwise take, that's a pressure tactic. When you say something because that is the way you feel about, that is a statement of fact. This becomes critical in online communication because, on the screen, the statements look exactly alike to the other person. If you run across a woman who accuses you of trying to

89

pressure her to make you feel guilty and keep you in a relationship that's going nowhere, make sure you know your motivation. Or, as Sergeant Friday used to say in *Dragnet*, "Just the facts, ma'am."

Who Pays the Telephone Bill?

This will be a short section—you do. I don't have to tell you how expensive telephone calls can be when they are long distance, or worse yet, international. Of course, if they're local, speaking to your online love over the phone will be much less expensive than speaking to her online. Be up-front with this potential lady of your dreams about how much money you are willing to spend on the phone and stick to it, even if you're independently wealthy. Any reasonable person understands the necessity of sticking to a budget; budgeting money is something you and she will no doubt do should your relationship evolve into a permanent physical-world one. Now is a good time to see if this person will be a supportive partner, or a spendthrift.

Be wary of a woman who demands that you call more often than you want to, even if she tells you how wonderful it is to hear your voice and she can just listen to it forever. Be wary also of a woman who seems to have all the money in the world to go online but pleads poverty when you suggest that she can pick up the phone and call, too. Where is she getting all that money? Is someone else paying for her online time, or does she just want to spend your money and her money on *her?* Either way, you may want to reassess the future of this potential relationship. If you find someone who is really reasonable, she may even volunteer to make an occasional call to you. Who knows? It can happen.

Be sure to continue to augment your telephone conversations with live online time, where the costs are shared, and e-mail, where you can get the most communication for your buck.

Telephone Jitters

Despite the fact that you may have been talking to this woman online for months and you'll be excited about finally hearing her voice, you may certainly get a severe case of nerves. That first telephone call, in many respects, is even more nerve-wracking than the first meeting. By the time you meet, your relationship will be pretty well established, and if things don't go well, you can always talk about the surrounding environment. "Hey, look at that tree! How old do you suppose it is?"

But a telephone call is just the two of you, strictly private. And unlike live chat where you can erase a word, or even retype your response before you send it, a telephone call is immediate. Once the words are out, you can't call them back. Worse even than the fear of saying something stupid is the fear of not having anything to say at all—the fear of the long, dead silence.

Keep in mind that she's feeling the same way. It's the first time she'll be speaking to you, too. Keep in mind also that this is the woman you've been speaking with online and you've never had a problem finding something to say to her. After some initial awkwardness, everything will be fine.

After you exchange phone numbers it's best to sign right off and call. If she sends you a message asking you if you're nervous, say, "Yes, but in a couple of minutes we'll be speaking to each other and then I won't be."

And just get on the phone.

No matter how long or short your online relationship has been, no matter how much or how little cybersex you've had, taking the step to voice is another level, and it really is like starting over. Approach your conversation with this in mind. Take the time to get to know her all over again. You might discuss the same things you discussed online, but this time it will be with a human female voice, complete with inflections, pauses, and breaths.

The online courtship can be the most wonderful experience a person can have. Where else but online can you get to know a woman all over again three times: Once online, once on the phone, and once in person? So, take it slow and get to know this wonderful woman on this new level of your courtship.

Talk Dirty to Me—Not!

Remember, you're not calling a phone-sex hotline when you make that first call to your online love. There can be no worse turn off on that first phone call than proving to her that all you've really been interested in all this time is sex. You kept sex in its proper perspective during your online relationship; keep it in its place on the phone. I realize the both of you may be really hot for each other at this point, but the first call, at least, should be reserved for verifying everything you've told each other and getting to know each other through this new medium.

Phone sex, like its counterpart, cybersex, needs to be kept in-bounds as you progress through this stage of your relationship. If the first phone call was successful, there will be many more before you finally meet your online love RT, and the temptation to engage in phone sex at some point will be considerable. After all, once you tell each other your life stories and discuss all your shared interests, what else is there? Those are things you can discuss with any friend, and this lady definitely has the potential of being more than a friend.

There is no question that during this stage of the relationship it's important to maintain a romantic element. As I mentioned in the chapter on cybersex, there is a difference between sensuality and sexuality. Just making a surprise call to her in the morning before you rush off to work and telling her that you woke up thinking about her says a lot more about you than any direct sexual comment ever could.

Telephone as Verification Tool

It's pretty remarkable how much background noise that telephone mouthpiece can pick up. I do believe that by the time you get to this stage you've developed a basic trust and the person you're dealing with is who she says she is, but hey, you never know. Be aware of background sounds that don't mesh with the picture you have of her. She said she lives in the 'burbs and you constantly hear the sound of sirens...hmm, must be a pretty busy night in suburbia. Hear a dog barking and she never mentioned having a dog? Conversely, pay attention to sounds that give you a better picture of her. Is the television on? The radio? What's playing? You might get a better idea of what her likes and dislikes are from these sounds. Listen up; play detective.

It also may surprise you to consider using the telephone to establish an identity that roots you firmly in a community apart from the online world. During a long telephone relationship I had with a beautiful lady I met online, we came to know not just each other but each other's friends and families. If I was out to dinner with friends, I would whip out the cellular phone, give her a call and say, "Hi, darling, I'd like you to say hello to so-and-so." She met a number of my friends and my mother this way and, likewise, I spoke to both her parents and her siblings. This added a level of reality and trust to our relationship and made the transition to meeting much easier and worry-free.

Now, you might be afraid of doing this for fear of being scoffed at by associates, "What, you met this woman on the computer? Are you nuts?" Well, the fact is meeting someone this way is a very acceptable thing to do—otherwise you and millions like you wouldn't be doing it, right? What's the worst that can happen? You'll meet and it won't work out. How many of your friends can boast of never having a relationship that didn't work out?

A Failed Connection

Not every call leads to romance. It would be nice, but that's just the way it is. It may be disappointing to realize the spark that existed and grew into a flame online just didn't carry over to the phone. Quite frankly, I don't believe this happens too often, unless you make the call too soon and there hasn't been time to develop a solid relationship. But, in essence, there really is no such thing as a failed communication. The purpose of this step is to test the waters in the process of actualizing the relationship in the physical world. If, for whatever reason, it doesn't seem as if it can progress any further, it is best to know it now so you can both move on without wasting each other's time.

Hopefully, the conclusion is mutual and, at the very least, you will remain friends and be grateful that, through this online medium, you have met someone whom you would not otherwise have met. Unfortunately, as is often the case in matters of the heart, the feeling is not mutual. I would hope that the both of you act maturely, discuss your feelings openly, and accept the other person's decision about the potential future of the relationship. If you don't, you can expect this woman will no longer speak to you, inform mutual online friends about your behavior who will come to her defense, and possibly report you to the online service management.

One should always keep in mind that anything that goes on on an online service goes on through a telephone line, and telephone lines are regulated by the Federal Communications Commission. So, getting reported to the online management can become a federal offense—and that can

93

mean an awful lot of trouble. It is much better to accept the other person's decision and move on. There is a woman out there who's just right for you and, with the help of this book, you will no doubt find her.

On the positive side, if this phone call goes well, you can be almost certain that you'll be meeting this woman, sooner rather than later. It is a risk worth taking.

Exchanging Photos

With the cost of scanning equipment dropping by the day, the availability of commercial scanning companies, and the fact that most major online services will now scan a photo for free and place it in the photo library, the exchange of photos between potential mates happens much more rapidly than it did just two years ago. In fact, I've had women e-mail me their photo within the first 20 minutes of meeting them online. You may, in fact, already have your photo in the photo library or on your home page and can simply direct a woman to view it.

This rapid exchange of photos may seem like a plus in discovering whether you want to continue evolving a relationship with that person, but it does have its drawbacks. Perhaps I'm an incurable romantic, but my views are shared by many people I've met online: The beauty of meeting someone online is that you can discover truly important connections without the interference of physical looks.

This must be true in general because, after all, it's not just the beautiful and handsome who get married, have kids, and live happily ever after. In fact, most people know that those physical traits fade with age and what's important are the emotional and intellectual connections. Exchanging photos too rapidly creates a barrier to finding out those more important aspects of the other person. Sure, you can exchange vital statistics fairly early on just to see if you're playing in the same ballpark, but that's not the same as seeing a photo.

It would also be a mistake to think that all the beautiful women online are anxious to parade their beauty in front of you. If anything, the opposite is true. Beautiful women get enough attention in the physical world—perhaps they're online to find a man who will love them for who they are on the inside and not for who they are on the outside. This is especially true in the case of public personalities, who could be recognized by their photos. These people too are perhaps looking for someone who will love them for who they are and not what they are.

94

Lastly, photos don't always tell the truth. Plenty of good looking people do not photograph well and vice versa. Photos can be out-of-date or, in extreme cases, not even be of the person you're talking to.

Whether or not you have a photo of yourself available online is strictly a matter of personal taste. But don't let the exchange of photos in the early stages of a potential relationship be the determining factor in pursuing the potential. If, when you exchange your vital statistics, the woman mentions she has a photo and asks if you'd like to see it, by all means say yes. But be assured that a point will be reached, usually when the two people decide they want to pursue the relationship further, that an exchange of photos will take place.

When that time comes, four things may happen:

◎ She may look better than she described herself.

◎ She may look exactly the way she described herself.

◎ She may not look the way she described herself.

◎ She may not send you a photo.

Obviously, the first two cases present no problem, except in the unlikely event she's a professional con person. In the last case, something is wrong and this potential relationship is probably over.

In the third case there is some question about what happened at the beginning. But let me hasten to add that before you get a photo that's substantially different from the description she's given you, she will probably hint strongly that her previous statements may not have been entirely accurate. Is this person a liar? We've already discussed the kinds of lies people tell online, some of them having to do with age and weight. So, it would not be surprising to find out that that person has exaggerated a wee bit about these topics. But there is another interesting thing that happens online.

It may be that when you first met that woman she had no interest in finding a mate, or she may have excluded you because of age or geographic location. But she liked the conversation and told you something she thought you would find appealing. Then something strange happened. She developed feelings; she fell in love, and she's stuck with that lie she told you. It would be nice if she had just told you as soon as she realized feelings were developing, but by then she was too afraid.

When the moment of truth comes in the exchange of photos, she breaks down and confesses. How you react is, of course, up to you but, personally,

95

if everything else has been going fine and there are no further inconsistencies in her story, I would let it pass. Sometimes a relationship is about accepting the weaknesses of others. As it is said, to err is human; to forgive divine. Don't allow a small foible to stop what could be an otherwise fulfilling and exciting relationship.

Romantic Actions

Your online relationship is going along fine. You are communicating on all sorts of levels: e-mail, live chat, telephone. What can be better than all this talk? Action, that's what. As the saying goes, actions speak louder than words. How about showing your online love you really are the romantic guy you say you are by sending her something special, if you have her address? There's nothing like receiving a surprise gift. It doesn't have to be anything expensive, just something that shows you're willing to put in a little extra effort. Some suggestions might be...

- A postcard of your town, on the back of which you may want to write, "This town is missing something—someone like you."
- A nice greeting card, the kind that says something like, "My life is so much better now that you're a part of it."
- A box of candy or a basket of fruit.
- Flowers, of course, are always in season and there is enough variety to fit anyone's wallet. What woman doesn't enjoy receiving flowers?

That first meeting 9

The decision to meet is often made even before both parties are fully aware of it. I like to think of it as a wave, far out to sea but destined to hit the beach; it doesn't *look* like a wave until it breaks and turns into all that frothy white stuff and you say, "Wow, that's a wave." So it is with the decision to meet. It's already out there but you don't notice it until it breaks into your consciousness and you find yourself saying, "Wow, we've got to meet."

The fact is, the decision to meet is often implied in that first solid online connection with someone you find special. It is definitely implied in that first successful phone call. As all the communication mounts, the wave is driving inexorably toward the beach and it's only a matter of time before you find yourself making plans to meet.

These are sometimes passionate plans, filled with the promise of a life of bliss. Maybe. But what's really important about this meeting is that this is the last transition of the online courtship process. This is when you'll put it all together and add all those missing physical elements: the body language, the facial expressions, the touch of a hand, a hug, perhaps a kiss or more.

No matter what your fantasies—or hers—may be, no matter how sexual and fantastic your online and telephone relationship has been, it's best to keep your goals firmly rooted in reality and practicality. Going into this meeting thinking that this is the beginning of the rest of your life with this person will place far too much pressure on both of you. This kind of pressure can doom the meeting before it even happens. It is much better to view it as just another step in the process.

Keeping Expectations Realistic

This is certainly an important meeting, but it's best to go into it with your head leading your heart, even if you've convinced each other that you're destined to be together. Up to now, as real as the relationship seems, it's still based strictly on fantasy and desire—emotions that can be far stronger than reality. You may in fact be everything you ever dreamed of to each other, but that still doesn't mean you'll be able to deal with the day-to-day things that occur in every relationship, the boring things, the mundane things, the annoying little habits each of us have. And even if this first meeting goes exactly as planned, you're still a long way from proving that you can tread life's hills and valleys together successfully.

So, keep it light, keep it fun, keep it realistic. Make sure you both understand that, whatever the outcome, you have each found someone with whom you can share your innermost feelings and feel comfortable. If it turns out there's no physical chemistry between the both of you, the qualities you've found in that person make the ingredients for a wonderful and lasting friendship. Make sure you both fully understand that it may not work out. More importantly, make sure you understand and discuss the possibility that one person may feel it went well but the other person does not. Make a commitment to her, and get a commitment from her, that, whatever the outcome, you will both continue to be friends.

By keeping expectations realistic, you'll really be open to getting to know this person all over again for the third time. There's no other courtship like it; make the most of it.

Making Plans

This is probably the first time you will plan an actual event together, and it can be complicated. It sure ain't like making plans to see a movie. Your online love may live quite a

98

distance away—across the country, or even be from another country. You may have to make sure passports are current, visas obtained, and, at the very least, travel plans arranged and confirmed. But, if you take everything step by step, making sure you're both in agreement at each step, things will go smoothly.

Who Goes Where?

Many online relationships are between people who live a great distance apart, so deciding who travels to whom is the first step. It's not always the case that the man travels to the woman's location, although you probably should, if no other arrangement can be reached. A lot of this really depends on whose schedule is more flexible. If you're a single dad, it might not be possible for you to get away even for a weekend.

A lot of it also depends on how far the relationship has progressed in terms of future plans should the first meeting work out. If you've talked about who would move where should this meeting go well, it makes sense for the person who would likely relocate to travel to the other person's hometown, even if that means it's the woman who travels. This way she'll get an idea of where you live and make some initial determination about whether she would want to live there.

If one person has an overriding fear about physical safety, then the other person should make the trip. This is a fear more associated with women than men, and the fact is, fewer men are victims of sexual crimes than women. If a woman voices these fears, don't get angry; understand where they're coming from. You may have had the longest and most trustworthy of online relationships, but this is a big step for her. Although logic may dictate she visit you, you may have to visit her.

I don't recommend meeting in a neutral city, especially if she has voiced concerns about physical safety. In fact, I would be concerned if a woman mentioned meeting in a neutral city; that sounds more like a tryst or an affair than a meeting between two people who want to have an RT relationship. Whatever city you decide on—yours or hers—you want this visit to be real, to get a sense of how the other person lives, to feel their roots.

Public or Private Meeting?

If the online relationship is long distance, the chances are good you'll initially meet in a public location. If you live in the same city or in close proximity to each other, you may wish to meet in a convenient public location like a restaurant.

99

The question isn't where you meet but where do you go *after* you meet? Now, I'm not going to be totally foolish and say you should go immediately from a public location to a private location, but I'm not going to be unrealistic and say it doesn't happen. In fact, it happens a lot more often than not.

Let's take a look at this situation practically. You are both adults. You've been speaking to each other online and on the phone for some time. If you've taken my advice about using the mail and the telephone as a verification tool, you already have a pretty good idea of who that person is. If you seriously think she's an ax murderer, what are you doing together? You better not pick her up from the airport in your car because three minutes after meeting her, you're going to be alone with her and she with you.

Unless you live within a couple of hours of each other, it's impossible to plan a meeting strictly around public places. If you're not prepared to be alone with this person, or she with you, forget meeting her. Neither one of you is ready.

How Long Do You Meet For?

The length of the meeting should be as short as practical depending on the distance you or she have to travel. For short distances (say, under 250 miles) or for places that can be reached by plane in under two hours, this meeting should last no longer than 5-6 hours. For longer distances, no more than a weekend. This strategy works well whether the meeting is everything you expected it would be or somewhat less. If the meeting is great, you'll both part with an increased desire and yearning for each other, which will, no doubt, make life after the meeting more full of excitement and expectation. If it didn't go well, you'll be grateful that it was as short as possible.

Spending the Night Together?

Maybe that's what you talked about during those sensuous conversations online and on the telephone, and maybe that's the way it will end up, but it would be presumptuous to assume that's what will absolutely, positively happen. Remember, this is the first time you're meeting f2f and you should keep your previous sensual relationship with this woman in its proper context. It's best for whoever's visiting the other to make reservations at a local hotel or motel, even if it turns out the maid doesn't have to make the bed in the morning.

Making Counterplans

No one goes into this meeting without high expectations, and while those expectations may be realized, that's not always the case. Even two people who appear to be ideally suited online and on the phone may find that the chemistry—sometimes elusive and impossible to define—just isn't there when they meet in person. While it may put a damper on otherwise hopeful meeting plans, discussing the possibility that things may not work out and deciding what to do if not should not be seen as negative or indicative of one party having second thoughts about meeting. Although unpleasant, this possibility should be discussed maturely and realistically.

Whatever the outcome, you have by now shared some pretty important personal stuff with each other. In most cases, you have communicated more to this person you haven't even met yet than to just about anyone in your RT world. Had you not developed such an in-depth relationship, you would not now be talking about meeting. At the very least, the things you've shared form the basis of a very real and close friendship. You should both decide before you meet that, whatever the outcome, you will maintain the friendship you have developed and that you will stay in touch. This is important not just because it's true but also because no one wants to feel they'll be forgotten just because one or both of you decide upon meeting that there is no potential for romance.

As the man, it also will be extremely important to assure the lady that her decision will be respected if she has no romantic interest in you but you have in her. It goes without saying that women feel more physically vulnerable than men. No matter how public you make this first meeting, the chances are very good that you will be alone together at some point. The situation is further complicated by the fact that your online and phone communication hasn't exactly been about the weather. She may be concerned that you will interpret the expectations surrounding the meeting and your previous communication as an automatic "Go" signal. Assure her that her no means "No." And make sure you have it straight in *your* mind and you're not thinking that her no might mean "Maybe" or "Yes" if you try a little harder. If you cannot assure her on this point, postpone the meeting.

Safety Considerations

Every day complete strangers meet in bars, clubs, shopping malls, museums, or even passing on the street. It is not uncommon for some of them, after a brief period of time, to end up alone, engaged in adult activity. Is there a risk involved in such a chance meeting? Absolutely. Yet, people do it.

Some risk is always involved in meeting a stranger for the first time. And to say there is none involved in meeting someone you met online for the first time would be foolhardy. But these risks are minimized by the fact that this is not a chance meeting; you have spent considerable time talking and making reality checks with that person. Still, taking proper precautions will make you feel more at ease and facilitate the growth of the feelings you began online.

◎ Make sure you verify his/her home address before leaving.

◎ Plan the itinerary of your trip down to the last detail and be wary if things suddenly change or do not appear to be as you were told. (For example, you can ask, "OK, you're going to pick me up at the airport and then we're going to drive to Joe's Italian Restaurant in town. What landmarks will I see on the way into town?" And then make sure you see them.)

◎ Meet in a public place, wherever possible.

◎ Plan to stay at a hotel or motel and make reservations beforehand. Hey, if you don't need them, things are probably going pretty good.

◎ Make sure that someone in your hometown knows exactly where you'll be and for how long, and give that person the address and phone number of the person you're visiting.

◎ Have pre-planned check-in times with your hometown contact.

Meeting Priorities

The moment of truth is at hand. Any anxiety, anticipation, or expectations disappear as you both stand f2f. Is there a moment of awkward silence? Probably not. You might first feel a sense of relief that the deed is finally done. After that, it's more like meeting an old friend with

102

whom you've shared many confidences than meeting a stranger. After all, you've been communicating with this person for quite some time. Conversation is easy and natural, and if that chemistry happens to be there, that first sight of your online love can be powerful indeed.

But, as I've said before, keep things in perspective—you're still a long way from a marriage proposal. Use this opportunity to interject that important element of reality into your relationship. Remember that online and on the phone it's much easier to hide flaws. Even if you've discussed them honestly, talking about them and witnessing them are entirely different. Of course, you won't be spending this valuable time looking for each other's warts. You'll be reaffirming all the connections you made in the previous two stages of this wonderful courtship. If all goes as planned, this third and final transition can be the beginning of a relationship that will last a lifetime.

The Meeting–An Assessment

It may seem rather cold and calculating to make a practical assessment of your meeting, especially if the emotions were as expected and you got along as if you've known each other forever. But love needs a solid foundation to survive and thrive. There are personal as well as practical issues to consider and, in some cases, discuss with her:

Is she everything she said she was? You've had a lot of discussions and most likely exchanged photos or given each other your description. Did she look like her photo or live up to her description? Keep in mind that there probably will be minor discrepancies between the way she looks in person and her photo; in most cases, you can probably discount those. What's really important are the things she said about her personality and character. Did she tell you she was the shy, retiring type but she's been nothing but garrulous and loud during the whole visit? If there appear to be some serious differences between the way she was online and on the phone and the way she is in person, you'll have to reassess this potential relationship in light of this new information.

Is she perfect except for _____ (fill in the blank)? If you can't accept her the way she is and find yourself thinking about all the changes you'd like to make in her, you should not start an RT relationship.

Did she appear to take care of her health? Did she drink just a little too much during dinner or any other time? Did she have drugs in her possession or ask you if you had any she could take?

Was the RT meeting everything you expected it to be? You both had a lot of hopes and dreams going into this meeting, based on virtual contact. Were you able to actualize those hopes and dreams during your meeting? If not, are the obstacles the product of some intrinsic personality conflict or were the hopes and dreams just unrealistic to begin with?

How much of the virtual relationship was carried over into the RT meeting? Sometimes the virtual relationship is so strong that it can mask basic differences that would have been apparent had not the virtual relationship preceded it. You may actually convince yourself that you're having an RT meeting when, in fact, you're still living a virtual one in your head. It's important to separate your RT meeting from everything that's gone before. After all, an RT relationship deals with RT issues, not virtual ones. Be as objective as possible with yourself and with her. If she meets any of your friends or relatives during her visit, don't be afraid to ask them their opinion of her and how you interacted with each other. Sometimes an outside observer can pick up something you missed, or confirm something you may already suspect.

How did you, or she, get along with the other person's friends and relatives? Wherever you may be planning to conduct your future RT relationship, you both have ongoing relationships with friends and relatives. If you're planning to move to her location, it's helpful if you like her friends and relatives and they like you. The same, of course, is true if she moves to your town. Friends and relatives play a role in every relationship, but they become more critical when one person has to relocate, possibly a great distance, and be in a new location without a support group.

Of course, we hope our friends and relatives will be supportive, but that isn't always the case. Friends and relatives can be extremely disruptive if they try to exclude your love or treat her coldly. On the other hand, she may not like your friends or relatives. This may lead her to attempt to separate you from them. Either situation can cause serious conflict in a new relationship.

What was your or her reaction to the location of the meeting? Since so many virtual relationships are long distance and involve the relocation of one party, it's important that the relocating person feel comfortable in his or her proposed new setting. If you've previously discussed the possibility of relocating, then you probably set this meeting in the city you or she would most likely relocate to.

104

A positive reaction to a person's surroundings will be important to the success of any future RT relationship.

Moving is considered one of the most stressful transitions a person makes. Relocating may involve a number of transitions, not just the obvious one of changing location and employment. For example, a person who is used to living in a house may find it difficult to change to an apartment. Look at and discuss all the transitions of moving from one location to another. You don't want to complicate a stressful situation with the added burden of one of you hating your new surroundings. If you didn't have this meeting in your proposed new location, I strongly suggest you set up a future meeting (or a few of them) there before you continue talking about making RT plans.

Life after the Meeting

You've really had a wonderful visit with your online love. Both of your expectations were not only met, they were exceeded. You both wish you could stay with each other a lot longer, maybe even forever, but individual responsibilities preclude that from happening at this point. So here you are, facing each other for a teary good-bye after what has been an all-too-brief meeting. Because of the distance between you, you both know it will be some time before you can see each other again.

Life after a successful meeting can be difficult. What once was a full, exciting online and phone relationship now appears hollow compared to being together RT. This is really as it should be. In light of a successful RT meeting, how can the virtual be anything but a shadow? Because of this there are two potential dangers in resuming a virtual relationship after an RT meeting. One is allowing the emotional letdown of going back to a virtual relationship to interfere with the genuine feelings you've developed for each other. The second is rushing into an RT relationship too quickly.

There are many ways to overcome the emotional letdown associated with going back to a virtual relationship. The most important is to keep in mind the completeness your virtual relationship now has. Although it may be sad not to be able to see your online love f2f, you should also be heartened that the voice on the other end of the phone now has physical form. When you receive an e-mail from her or speak to her, imagine the expression on her face as you remember her. By using your imagination, your virtual relationship may be even better than before.

The other thing to keep in mind is that you will see each other again, and any RT plans you make for the future will be based in fact and not fantasy. Finally, it's important to maintain that element of romance that you achieved during your online courtship. Don't let the emotional blahs make you blasé. Keep the sensual element in your e-mail letters and telephone calls. Tell her you miss her. Send flowers. As a matter of fact, send flowers as soon as you can after you meet her.

While it is important to maintain the romance after a successful meeting, it is equally important to use this time after the meeting to reflect upon it in the cool light of reason. (This is a good time to ask yourself some of those questions I listed in the assessment section earlier.) It's very important to not allow yourself to get carried away in the heat of the moment. One thing to watch out for is either one of you trying to compensate for missing the other person with increased phone calls. That can become very expensive. Make a phone budget and stick to it. It'll be good practice on working together, which will be important to the success of a possible RT relationship.

Once you give yourselves time to reflect and come to a mutual decision that you want to proceed, you can begin to make practical plans about future meetings and a possible RT relationship. Keep in mind, however, that one successful meeting doesn't necessarily guarantee a lifetime of happiness.

Do You Continue to Meet Others in RT?

It's obvious that if you decide she's not right for you, you'll have to tell her that and continue your search. If you've been dating more than one woman online, you'll make plans to meet another woman. If you had a mutually successful meeting and you haven't been dating others, then it doesn't seem like you'd want to to meet any other women. But if either of you were having multiple virtual relationships, do you continue to arrange RT meetings with other women even if you feel the meeting was successful?

Of course, what you ultimately decide will be based on your feelings towards the woman you met, in your sound and reasonable judgment, and should be discussed with her. Listed below are some guidelines you will want to consider in making your decision:

◎ Meet the other women if you've both been having multiple virtual relationships and mutually decide you want to meet the others before you make a final decision.

◎ Meet the other women if you feel it's necessary for you to make a final decision, even if she doesn't want to meet any other men. In this case, of course, she should be aware that you were dating other women online while you were dating her, and you should have already mentioned to her you want to meet the others.

This can become a difficult situation and a cause for conflict. Keep in mind that this is not a game and you will not start *new* virtual relationships with the intention of meeting other women. Make sure you're very definite about the time you'll need to make a decision and stick to it. Of course, you'll also tell the other women about your decision and will have already told them you've met a woman RT. You better be good at explaining things if you go this route!

◎ Meet the other women if she has unilaterally decided she wants to meet the other men she has been dating online. This is the same situation as above, except in reverse. Don't be a martyr. If she wants to meet the other men she's been dating, be magnanimous and give her the time and space she needs to make a decision. If you are truly meant for each other, it won't take her long to figure that out.

The Move Towards Permanence

Keep in mind that one meeting does not a relationship make. Despite your love for each other, many steps must still be taken, not the least of which is figuring out the often-complicated arrangements of consummating a long distance relationship. Before you even talk about making it permanent, you really must ask *yourself* if this is the person you want to spend the rest of your life with. After all, you or she will most likely have to move, and a failed relationship of this type not only involves hurt feelings but great inconvenience to the one who moves. That person has often given up a job, friends, and family and moved to unfamiliar surroundings, so it is critical that both of you are as sure as possible that the relationship will work.

You should plan to spend considerable time with each other before making a decision of this magnitude, to make sure the basics of a long-term relationship exist. While no one can determine the power of love to overcome obstacles, experts agree that the basics of a good long-term relationship include:

Truthfulness   Does she lie to you or others?

Reliability   Does she keep her appointments and is she where she says she's going to be?

Responsibility   Does she take good care of herself and the things she claims are important to her, such as pets and plants?

Financial prudence   Does she constantly go over her credit limit?

Stability   Can she keep friends and does she have a good relationship with parents?

Faithfulness   Would you ever be concerned that she might cheat on you?

In most RT relationships, the preceding qualities are about all you'll need to consider before making a decision. But because so many online relationships are long distance, there will be some practical questions involved in the move towards permanence. Let's take a look at them next.

The Practical Considerations

Who moves?

Who pays for the move?

These questions have nothing whatsoever to do with love. You should decide them in the most practical and logical manner possible.

In most cases, the question of who moves is more a financial decision than an emotional one. Usually, the person with the lower paying job moves to the hometown of the person with the higher paying job. However, there can be extenuating circumstances to consider when making this decision. Some low-salaried jobs have more career potential than some high-salaried jobs. In that case, you may want to make a decision

108

based on the future earning potential of a particular position rather than its present salary. Some jobs are more universally marketable than other jobs, regardless of salary. In that case, the person with the more marketable position may find it easier to make the move.

There are other things to consider besides income. One or both of you may have school-age children. It's not easy to uproot children. If one has children and the other doesn't, the one who doesn't may have to make the move. One of you may be faced with caring for elderly or infirm parents. One or both of you may own a house. You'll need to determine whose house has the best market rental value and discuss the problems of being an absentee landlord, possibly living quite a distance from the property. (I do not recommend selling anything at this point.)

All of these considerations must be thrown into the mix and discussed before you can reach any rational conclusion. It might be a good idea to make a list, independent of each other, ranking your priorities in order of importance, and then compare the lists. Certainly, you need to work out any serious conflicts before either of you makes a move. The question of who pays for the move is more detailed than it may appear. A move is far more complicated than the physical act of packing some boxes and shipping them from point A to point B. You'll need to allow time for the person who's moving to settle in and become familiar with a new environment, and realize that person may be without an income for a while. If at all possible, the relocating party should have reasonable assurance of a job before the move is made, but that isn't always possible.

It's my feeling that no matter who pays for the physical move, the financial burden of the transition period should be shared by both parties. Unless one person is clearly capable of supporting the other, it would be completely unfair to ask either party to bear this expense alone. There can be nothing more detrimental to a new relationship than to have it run into serious financial difficulty a few weeks after the move. Since you are starting a new relationship, it seems reasonable for both parties to bring adequate financial resources to the table to give this relationship a chance to succeed.

This doesn't mean that the person who is not moving has no further responsibilities. Indeed, the opposite is true. If she is the one who moved, don't think that now that she's here you've "got her" and can stop paying her the attention you showed during your courtship. That attention is why she moved in the first place, and don't think she'll settle for anything less just because it's too difficult to move back. Nothing could be further from the truth.

You have tremendous responsibility in making sure she feels entirely welcome in her new surroundings. You need to be very supportive; recognition of the sacrifice she has made is critical. You should take time off from work to be with her as much as possible, and make every attempt to incorporate her into your circle of family and friends. Remember, she will have no support group in her new location, and moving is a traumatic experience. Finally, if things don't work out, you should bear some of the financial burden of moving her back.

And if *you're* the one who moved, you should settle for nothing less from her.

Of course, it all sounds nice, neat, and logical when looked at from an objective point of view. But love isn't always neat and logical. We'll take a look at some people who took a chance on love in the next chapter. Don't be surprised that not all of them did it the nice, neat, and logical way.

They took the R•T RISK

Throughout this book, we've talked about the ways you can meet a woman online and develop a relationship with her. The purpose has been, of course, to help you find that woman of your dreams and to facilitate crossing the bridge from the virtual to RT. I think, therefore, that it's appropriate to end this book by meeting some people who took that risk and are better people for it.

I've tried to find stories that are realistic, so not all of the stories you're about to read are "happily ever after" stories. We're adults and we all know that those stories only happen in fairy tales. In real life, things don't always work out the way we planned. Meeting someone online doesn't guarantee that your RT relationship will have a better chance than meeting a woman at the museum or the supermarket. The important thing is that you take the chance on love. As Shakespeare once said, "It is better to have loved and lost, than never to have loved at all."

Still, although these stories are not fairy tales, there is a fairy-tale element here. It is the computer. Because without that computer attached to a modem connected to an online service, none of these people would have ever met. There was no chance they could have bumped into each other walking down the street. And, therefore, they would have never experienced each other and would have never enjoyed each other. The computer as participant in a fairy tale? It seems strange, but, yes, it's true. For millions of people, the computer now plays a part in our destiny. Here are the stories of five of those people:

They Met within Four Days

Frank, an actor, was emotionally dead inside. While he could easily feign all the emotions necessary to be convincing on stage, and he was certainly in a position to meet some very attractive women, he could not bring himself to take the steps to form a relationship. In fact, he hadn't had a relationship in eight years.

He joined an online service because he owned a computer and a disk with ten free hours for the service came in a computer magazine he bought. He was a member of the online service for six months, paying $9.95 per month for five hours he never used. One day he decided that, since he was paying for it, he would at least use the five hours per month. He spent a couple months investigating all the facets of the service and found some interesting things. There were magazines to read, files to download, and company profiles to investigate.

At some point he found the service's chat area. It didn't seem that appealing at first but, apparently, a lot of people thought it was—there were always so many people in all those rooms. So, he kept going back, never actually going into a room, but looking from afar, so to speak, at all the people in them. One room of all the thousands did attract his attention, however, and one night he went into it. He didn't speak to anybody—didn't even say hello—but he liked what he saw. People seemed to be having fun.

One lady in particular caught his eye. She seemed outrageously flirtatious, but also very intelligent, and her high-energy antics made her the center of attention. He didn't speak to her, but he did check her profile. That night, after he signed off, he composed an e-mail letter to her, introducing himself, thanking her for being so entertaining, and mentioning that they had a number of things in common. When he signed on the very next morning, he was thrilled to find an e-mail letter from her—the first e-mail he had ever received. The letter was beautifully written and quite long, inviting him to contact her again.

When he signed on at 11:00 that night she was also online, and he sent her a private message. By the time they said good-night, it was 6 a.m. His fingers ached from all that typing, but the rest of him felt energized. From that moment on, they were an online item. Although she was still rather popular, when Frank came on and messaged her, she would give him her sole attention. They would spend 20 hours a week online together, and write two or three e-mail letters a day to each other. As the weeks progressed, he found long-dead emotions stirring in him. He wanted to meet this woman who did something to him that no RT woman had done in years but, alas, she refused. Refused even to exchange phone numbers.

After a couple of months of trying to get her to change her mind, he reluctantly gave up the relationship. But something had happened to Frank in that time. Thanks to his computer and the woman he met through it, he felt alive again, felt he wanted the warmth and tenderness of a woman next to him, and felt the need to share a life with someone again. He also realized the potential of the computer to accomplish that goal. He had become quite an online pro in those months. He knew the chat rooms well and knew which ones had the most potential for meeting a woman who shared his interests. He also became acquainted with many of the regulars, had spoken to some of them over the phone, and had even met one or two of them in RT.

So, after that first failed online relationship, Frank used his online contacts and found out about a woman who was looking for an RT relationship. Like his first online contact, he had seen Nancy in the chat rooms but had never spoken to her live. One afternoon he saw her in their regular room and was about to speak to her, but, before he could, she signed off. Frustrated at not taking the opportunity to speak when he could, he struck up a conversation with another woman. After a few weeks he met her RT when she had reason to travel to his hometown. Although she was physically everything she said she was, they realized there was no electricity between them and they parted as friends.

The next Saturday he signed on and saw Nancy. Not wanting to miss another opportunity to speak with her, he immediately messaged her, using the service's private messaging system. He knew she would recognize his screen name from the room so his message to her was, "It seems I know a lot more about you than you know about me." To which she responded, "Hmm. Would I want to know as much about you as you

113

THEY TOOK THE RT RISK

know about me?" Frank went on to explain what he knew about her and how he came to know it, and told her about himself. After an hour's conversation online, she gave him her phone number.

Their first telephone conversation lasted over four hours and they discussed many topics. She was three years younger than he. Being from the same generation, they had many things in common from their past, and, as it turned out, in general. Over the next few days, they spoke on the phone constantly and became quite eager to meet each other. Since they lived only 200 miles apart, the distance wasn't insurmountable, but their busy schedules could not be reconciled for weeks.

Finally, he said, "What are you doing today?"

"Talking to you," she replied.

"Well, why don't you make reservations on the train for me while I jump in the shower; I can take any train after 12 p.m."

It was 10:30 a.m. at the time.

He arrived at the railroad station in her hometown at 4 p.m. They had told each other what each would be wearing. When he arrived, no woman there matched her description, but after 20 minutes, he noticed a woman walk by who did. Not sure if it were her or not, he waited a short distance from her until he could catch her attention. She turned and looked at him and he knew she had to be the one. She approached him. They gazed into each other's eyes, then kissed deeply. For the next six hours they frolicked hand-in-hand in her hometown, stealing kisses in restaurants, on the street, and in her house. Then it was time for him to go, but although the meeting had been brief, it was electric and full of hope.

Over the next few weeks they spoke daily on the phone and traveled to visit each other regularly. Within five weeks of their first meeting, he moved to her hometown to live with her.

Virtual relationship: 4 days
RT relationship: 1 year
Current status: Living together

Small-Town Girl Moves to Big City

Steven wasn't really looking for a relationship when he happened across a woman alone in a chat room. He had enough online experience to know that a woman alone in a chat room was unusual. After all, wherever a woman went online, the men were sure to follow. That in itself was intriguing; perhaps she had just created the room and it hadn't yet been discovered? He decided to ask and sent her a private message.

She responded that she was a bit sad because her online relationship wasn't going well. Since he'd had a number of previous online relationships and even one RT relationship, he understood the feelings that develop between people sight-unseen. As it turned out, she, too, had considerable online experience, so their first conversation was about finding love online. She told him her name was Simone. When they said good-night a couple of hours later, he hoped that she felt a little better. It had been a nice conversation, but they made no plans to meet again.

Once that initial contact was made, however, it seemed as if they bumped into each other quite a lot online. Each time they did, they spoke, and each conversation uncovered something else they had in common. Although they always had nice conversations, she wouldn't consider starting another relationship until she met the man she was currently seeing online in RT. That meeting was scheduled some months in the future. Although Steven was a little miffed, he realized that he was dealing with an especially honest person and said that he would contact her again in a few months, without really having much intention of doing so.

Still, when he saw her online, he said hello and asked how her relationship was going and if she had met her virtual fellow in RT yet. Although each meeting was brief, he realized that he liked this woman's qualities. And, since they were in the same line of work, they also developed a professional rapport.

Eventually the man she was seeing online came to visit her. When Steven asked about the visit and she responded, "I think we could be friends," he knew their meeting hadn't gone well. But he never expected to have an RT relationship with this woman—too many things were against it. She was from the West Coast; he was from the East Coast. She was from a small town; he was from a big city. Nonetheless, they exchanged photos and an online relationship developed. Soon she felt comfortable talking with him over the phone.

Once they began speaking over the phone, a relationship, in all its virtual aspects, developed. Often their conversations lasted four to five hours. Phone bills grew to astronomical proportions, often topping $1,000 per month. But they did find out a lot about each other during their conversations. One of the most important things they both say they discovered was that the other person seemed very reliable and dependable. He always called when he said he would and she was always there to receive his call. They also continued to write plenty of e-mail to each other, in which they found themselves very compatible and responsive to each other's thoughts.

"To say that there was a lot of communication going on between us would be an understatement," Simone says.

In addition, Simone spoke to a couple of Steven's friends when he called her from his cellular phone, so even though she didn't know these people, she at least knew that there were other people in his life who knew him and could vouch for him. He also had occasion to speak to her mother.

After a couple of months of "voicing," they decided to meet. She had never been to his hometown; in fact, she had never even been to the East Coast. He made reservations for her to arrive on Friday evening and to depart on Sunday evening, and sent her the airplane tickets.

Despite all of the communication, there was a lot of anxiety surrounding that first visit. Coming 3,000 miles to meet a man she had never met was frightening enough by itself, but coming to a city she had never seen added to the tension. They had spent so much money on telephone calls and airline tickets that there wasn't enough for hotel reservations, so she would be spending that first weekend in Steven's apartment.

What if she hated him? What if he hated her? Would he just leave her at the airport to fend for herself? He had assured her that, no matter what the outcome, they had enough common interests to have a pleasant weekend and they would at least part as friends. Still, it was risky. For a while, he thought she would back down at the last minute and resigned himself to losing the price of the plane tickets.

But she didn't back down, and that Friday evening, as planned, she stepped off the airplane, out of the virtual world into the RT one. That first weekend was fantastic but all too brief. They got along famously in every way.

"It was like meeting someone for the first time [yet whom] you already knew," she says.

116

After that first meeting, their long-distance relationship took on a new perspective. In so many ways it had been enhanced. When he called her, each knew exactly what the other person looked like; the voice at the other end had dimension. She knew what he meant when he said he was sitting on the couch. The details that were only spoken of and described before were now real, and they both could picture them. It wasn't long before they wanted to see each other again.

The next time she came to visit him, a few months later, it was for six weeks. This time it was more like real life, since he had to work. She even brought her dog. Still, that six weeks went by too quickly. Then she was gone again.

This time, their long-distance relationship was not enhanced by her visit. They both felt the loss and separation deeply.

"She really added a lot to my life in those six weeks and I wanted her to be with me in real time."

She felt the same way. While they spoke every night, there was a certain hollowness to it, a touch of falseness.

It wasn't long before they were making plans to live together. Since circumstances made it more difficult for him to move, they decided that she would move permanently to the East Coast. Still, her life was not so easily packed in a bag and shipped, so there were many hurdles to overcome. After months of planning, arranging, and getting her life in order on the West Coast, she arrived at the airport where she had been twice before. This time, though, it was to be permanent. Still, a return ticket was purchased—just in case.

As it turned out, the big city was too much for this small-town girl, and so was the separation from her family on the West Coast. After close to a year of trying to acclimate herself, she decided to use that return ticket before it expired and go back to her more familiar and comfortable surroundings. Their life together was good and the airport that had so many times been a place of joy and hope now seemed dismal and depressing as they said their good-byes. Steven waited in the airport until her plane took off, hoping that she would change her mind—that, somehow, the plane would return to the gate and she would be back. When the plane became a disappearing speck in the Western sky, he turned from the window and walked alone back to his car.

When Simone arrived in her hometown she was warmly greeted by her family. Although thrilled to see them and happy to be back in familiar surroundings, she knew as soon as she stepped off the plane that something important was missing. All the family and all the familiarity didn't make up for the need she felt for Steven.

On the East Coast, Steven felt the same. As the weeks progressed, their feelings of loss and sadness didn't diminish. In fact, both of them felt worse the longer they were apart. After three months of being apart, she called him one Sunday morning and announced that she was coming back. Steven was overjoyed. So, for the fourth time, she packed her belongings and shipped them back to Steven's apartment. The airport once again became a joyous place as she stepped off the plane to start a new life—all over again.

Virtual Relationship: 8 months
RT Relationship: 1 year
Current status: Engaged

A Lie Almost Destroyed Their Love

Paul, a local sportscaster, had to put on a happy face when he appeared before the cameras. But inside he was very unhappy. His marriage of 30 years had long since disintegrated. He and his wife had become strangers to each other. He had tried to put it back together many times, but after years of trying, he had given up and resigned himself to living out the rest of his life in misery.

When he started signing on to an online service and discovered the chat areas, he saw it as a place where people played games and had fun. Paul had become so separated from his feelings and his own reality that he didn't see the connection between the names that popped up on his computer screen and the living people behind those names. To him, it was just one big fantasy where real feelings didn't exist, where no one could get hurt, and where he could escape from his loneliness and despair.

Consequently, when he spoke to a woman online, he never told them he was married. In fact, he would tell women he was *not* married. He wasn't the type to lie in real life, but this was a game, right? For the most part, it didn't matter—he wasn't looking for love, he just wanted to speak to other people, to connect, to play. He had never cheated on his wife and he was certainly not interested in a cyber-affair. For him, it was just harmless talk.

118

One day he found himself in a chat room with a number of people from Indiana. As he watched the conversation scroll by, the subject of the famous Indianapolis 500 race came up and various people offered their opinions about it. This got his sportscaster's attention. One woman, Beth, typed that she loved the race and went every year. That got Paul's attention, and he messaged her privately telling her that he loved the race also and, in fact, was there the previous year and wouldn't it have been funny if they were only a couple of rows apart? And so began another conversation with another woman, much as they had begun before.

Except this one would turn out to be different. Little by little, their short conversations turned into longer ones. They found they had a lot in common.

"She was such a real person to me," says Paul, "I just didn't know such a connection could be made."

As the days progressed, Paul found himself looking for Beth when he signed on and talking to her exclusively. She told him about her own unhappy and abusive marriage of 12 years. He found himself identifying with her situation—without, of course, ever mentioning his own similar circumstances.

Although they were becoming closer, Paul never made any commitment to meet Beth online at any specific time. Their meetings were serendipitous, but they did always seem to be online at the same time. It seemed as if they were being drawn together by an unseen force. Between meetings, there would be the occasional e-mail. After a few months of speaking online, Paul gave Beth his office phone number.

In spite of himself, Paul found that he was developing real feelings for Beth. At first those feelings were in the form of a deep friendship, a friendship that helped Beth see the futility of staying in a bad marriage and got her to take the initial steps toward getting out of it.

But underneath, stronger emotions were developing—emotions Paul hadn't felt for many years. He recognized love among them. And therein was the problem. How could he continue to make believe he was not married? How could he rectify the lie that he had so unwittingly and naively told? He now saw the person behind the screen name, understood that a lie told to an unseen person could hurt. He felt he loved Beth as a person and knew he couldn't keep lying to her. He tried many times to tell her but he couldn't do it because now he was also afraid to lose her. He was stuck in a lie, and the lie was hurting him.

Paul was not the only one developing feelings. Beth, too, was falling in love. He was so different from her husband. He was supportive; he was respectful; he made her laugh; he was what she wanted. Although everything seemed perfect, Beth felt something was very much amiss. Something about the times he signed on suggested that his time was constrained by something more than work. To her that could only mean that he was married or was living with someone.

Being a direct person, Beth asked him the next time they found each other online. Now, faced with the choice of finally telling the truth or continuing the lie, Paul found he could do neither. He was paralyzed into inaction and changed the subject. Beth did not press the issue but her suspicions were confirmed. A short time later Beth called Paul at the office. A teen-age boy answered the phone. When she asked for Paul, she heard the young man say, "Dad, it's for you."

What followed was a very painful but cleansing conversation. In tears, Paul unburdened himself of the terrible lie he had been hiding. Although he had yet to meet her, he told her she was the most special person he had ever met and that he was sure he wanted to be with her. She let him speak, then she told him that she had suspected he was married and that she loved him too.

The truth gave Paul new strength and determination. He finally had a direction and purpose. Within a few days of that phone call, Paul told his wife that their marriage was a sham and that he wanted a divorce. He then got in his car, drove to the airport and flew to Beth's home in Indiana.

That first meeting was everything they expected it to be. Beth says: "When we met each other that first time, we knew we loved each other. The first meeting was passionate, emotional, loving, and caring—everything we knew it would be."

"In Beth, I found love, a lover, and a friend," Paul says. "I'm 53 years old and I never new what love was until I found Beth. I learned an important lesson, one that will, no doubt make this relationship even more successful: If you are looking for someone you want to become close with, you better be truthful."

Paul and Beth see each other as often as they can now. Both are proceeding with their divorces, and Beth plans to move to his hometown as soon as they become final.

Virtual Relationship: 6 months
RT Relationship: 6 months
Current status: Planning marriage

120

They Talked about the Weather

Jack, a computer programmer, was quite familiar with online services and had been a subscriber for a few years. He signed on to read magazines, download files, and pick up his e-mail. He had met a number of interesting men and women in the chat areas and enjoyed corresponding with them via e-mail. Although he wrote to some women, those relationships were strictly platonic.

In fact, he was not interested in meeting a woman online. His RT world already included a couple of ladies whom he was dating. While neither relationship was serious or likely to become so, he was quite happy with his present circumstances. And, if the truth were told, he didn't really believe what the women online told him about their physical appearance. He liked the idea of being able to see a woman before he got emotionally involved. As friends, they were fine, but as potential lovers...that was another thing all together. So, when he did go into the chat area he never went into any of the rooms that could be considered "pick up" rooms, and when he happened to speak to a woman, he kept his conversations neutral.

Suzanne loved the chat rooms and she loved to flirt. Having just gone through an emotionally draining divorce, she saw the rooms as a way to release her still-considerable tension, and a safe place to flirt without getting emotionally involved. She never had to make much effort because as soon as she entered a chat room, plenty of men immediately messaged her privately and off she'd go into some flirtatious new encounter.

She had seen Jack in the chat room they both frequented on many occasions and always liked the comments he typed into the room, but they had never spoken. He had never once messaged her! In fact, she was a little miffed that he hadn't done so in all this time. He seemed intelligent and a good person to flirt with. So, one night when he entered, she typed into the room, "Hello, Jack." Much to her surprise and delight, he responded with a typed hello, almost immediately followed by a private message asking her about the weather. Her first thought was, "The weather?! He's asking me about the weather?!"

She told him it was sunny and warm. He replied that it was snowing where he lived. She said that she loved the snow and, as flirtatiously as she could get discussing the weather, asked if he would bring her some.

And that's how it all began. Although their conversation remained neutral, something had clicked in that inexplicable way things do when a connection is made. Suzanne found herself telling him about the real things that were going on in her life instead of engaging in the more superficial patter she had become accustomed to with men.

"Everything felt so natural with him; something very real happened in that conversation," she says.

Jack felt exactly the same way about Suzanne. Much to his amazement, the idea that he needed to know what the woman looked liked didn't seem so important. In fact, the subject of physical appearance never even came up.

"I had spoken to quite a few women online but there was something very different about Suzanne," he says.

When it was time to say good night, he asked her if she would be online again the following evening, and she said she would. It was the first time Jack ever asked that question, and the first time she had ever confirmed with a man that she would be there for him again.

After only five hours of speaking online, Jack asked for her phone number. By any online standard, five hours is a very short time in which to ask for a woman's phone number. Jack did worry that he would be turned down and wondered if this flickering flame of a relationship would be quickly extinguished by an ill wind. But he put any thoughts of defeat out of his mind and plunged ahead. He stared at his computer screen waiting for what he hoped would be a positive response.

When the unexpected question came via private message, Suzanne was taken aback, but only for the briefest moment. Any trepidation she felt about giving Jack her phone number so soon was negligible in comparison to the depth of feeling that had grown between them in those five hours. If he turned out to be someone entirely different over the phone, the worst thing that could happen would be that she would need to change her phone number. So, like Jack, she put all doubts aside and messaged back her phone number. Interestingly, they still had not exchanged physical descriptions.

That first conversation lasted longer than the entire time they had spent together online to that point. They had so many things in common, so many things to talk about, it was difficult to end the conversation. Over the next four months, there would be many more telephone conversations, e-mail and time spent online together.

At some point they did describe their physical appearance to each other, but it was long past the time when looks seemed to matter. The idea of exchanging photographs never even occurred to them, but Suzanne recalls that it didn't seem important. Their relationship had been cemented along the more important lines—the emotional, intellectual, and spiritual. They shared an openness that neither of them had experienced with any other person. "We just didn't have any secrets from each other," says Jack.

After a short time, he knew he had to meet her and drove out to do so. That was four months after they met online.

"We were both a little nervous, but there were no anxieties," he says. "There was no question that the online relationship that was established would work when we met."

As it turned out, it very much did. They saw each other regularly for the next three months. One weekend Suzanne came for a visit and Jack proposed. The following Monday, Suzanne gave her two-week notice at work and packed her belongings. Although good-byes to friends and family were sad, the promise of a happy life propelled Suzanne onward. When she stepped off the plane in Jack's hometown two weeks later, she was met by a limousine and whisked directly to the chapel where they were married.

Online relationship: 4 months
RT relationship: 3 months
Current status: Married one year

afterword

e started this book with the idea that it is possible, and even desirable, to find the right woman using a computer connected to an online service, and ended it with some stories of people who did it. Along the way we've discussed the various ways and means you can use to find the woman of your dreams, form a virtual relationship with her, and successfully move that relationship through the telephone and meeting stages.

Personally, I never stop marveling at the enthusiasm of the people I've spoken to who have found real happiness this way. Maybe it's because I, too, found happiness using a computer. But I think the enthusiasm is also part awe at the miracle of the method. When you think that you can find someone who is just perfect for you, someone you would never, ever have had the possibility of meeting in RT, you have to consider it a miracle. And really, that's what it is: a miracle you can make happen for yourself. I hope you've found this book valuable to your search. Most of all, I hope you saw this book as a guide to the possible and it convinced you to make the miracle happen for yourself.

If you'd like to find out more about this book and finding love online, visit Macmillan's World Wide Web page at **http://www.mcp.com/mgr**.

About the Author...

Richard M. Rogers lives in New York City with his girlfriend Karen and their three-year-old miniature pinscher, Casey.

index

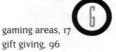